Readers praise Catherine Galasso-Vigorito's writing:

Leo Gross of Bismarck, North Dakota: "I am writing to compliment you on your excellently written column. Not only do you write well, but . . . your message is profound. I have now read the column four times, and each time I am able to get more out of it. I am going to frame it and hang it in my office."

Sheila M. Bartlett, King of Prussia, Pennsylvania: "I was drawn to your article immediately and found it so terrific . . . I truly believe you have so much to offer. I hope and pray you will continue to be the inspiration to the world that you already are becoming."

Laurie Arthur, Cheshire, Connecticut: "Thank you for putting such decent, truthful, and moral messages in the newspaper. Your articles are the best news conveyed in the newspaper—they should be on the front page of all the newspapers in our country . . ."

Cheryl Sylvia, Taunton, Massachusetts: "I read your column and the contents reach out and touch my heart . . . almost as if you wrote it just for me. I have been sharing your gift of writing with my family and friends. I make copies, bring them to work, and hang them on my refrigerator. You are truly beautiful and unique."

Art and Bea Chaput, Pawtucket, Rhode Island: "Thank you so much for your wonderful articles. May you continue to be led by God's Hand and may He continue to inspire you to write these thought-provoking and life-changing articles."

Janet Lynch, New Braunfels, Texas: "I keep all of your articles in a binder and hope to pass them on to my children someday. People like you make the world a better place."

A
NEW YOU

Words to Soothe the Mind, Body, and Spirit

Catherine Galasso-Vigorito

ADAMS MEDIA CORPORATION
Avon, Massachusetts

Published by
Adams Media Corporation
57 Littlefield Street, Avon MA 02322. U.S.A.
www.adamsmedia.com

ISBN: 1-58062-757-9

Printed in Canada.

J I H G F E D C B A

Library of Congress Cataloging-in-Publication Data
Galasso-Vigorito, Catherine.
A new you / by Catherine Galasso-Vigorito.
p.   cm.
ISBN 1-58062-757-9
1. Christian life. I. Title.
BV4501.3.G35 2002
248.4--dc21
2002009814

Cover photograph ©Natural Selection/Orion.
Border art by Kathie Kelleher.

This book is available at quantity discounts for bulk purchases.
For information, call 1-800-872-5627.

For the unconditional love, unwavering support, and genuine kindness so freely given, I dedicate this book to my husband, Todd.

And to our two darling daughters, delightful Lauren Grace and our littlest angel, Gabriella Elise, that they may catch hold of this comforting faith and joy of life.

Acknowledgments

"I do not cease to give thanks for you, remembering
you in my prayers."—Ephesians 1:16.

Everyone who accomplishes something extraordinary has had
divine encouragement from someone. God sends His people to be
a positive influence, a pillar of strength, a source of comfort and of hope
to another.

With all my heart, I thank God for the special individuals who have
tremendously influenced my life. And I thank Him for using me to
encourage others with the encouragement that I was given.

My greatest gratitude I owe to my eternal friend, mentor, and second
mother, Sylvia Jackson. Many of her words of unconditional love and
sixty-two years of wisdom are passed along to you in these essays. Her
faith has daily touched my life with grace and wonder. She is a true gift
from God, a treasure beyond words. I love you.

My heartfelt thanks to the extremely gracious and kind Executive
Editor Claire Gerus of Adams Media, whose belief in my abilities, so gen-
erously given, means more than I could ever express. And to the talented
staff at Adams Media, including Bob Adams; Publicity Director Carrie
Lewis McGraw; Publicist Gene Molter; Director of Sales and Marketing
Amy Collins; Director of Sales for Mass and Gift Markets Matt Gildea;
Managing Editor Kate McBride; Copy Chief Laura MacLaughlin; Art
Director Paul Beatrice; Production Director Sue Beale; Assistant Editor
Kate Epstein; Publishing Director Gary Krebs; and Internet Manager
Greg Almeida, for their enthusiasm and vision, and for enfolding me with
such warmth.

For her top-notch professionalism and consideration to me, I want
to express my appreciation to Anne Sellaro of Anne Sellaro Associates.

I would like to extend my gratitude wholeheartedly to the Journal Register Company Chairman, President, and CEO, Robert M. Jelenic; Executive Vice President, Chief Financial Officer, and Secretary Jean B. Clifton; and Charles S. Pukanecz, Vice President, News; who continued to recognize what is of the utmost importance in journalism.

Thank you to William J. Rush, former publisher of the New Haven *Register*, and to his lovely wife, Ruth, who gave me the unusual opportunity to share my talents and love for God. I have received letters from all over the world commending a newspaper company for publishing such a faith-filled column.

To the publisher of the New Haven *Register*, Kevin Walsh, and my dear friend, Executive Assistant Ann Marie Brennan, your prayers, genuine warmth, and caring has meant the world to me. I am blessed to call you friends.

My appreciation to Dan Barger, publisher of the Monroe County Journals, for his dedication and support.

My thanks to Raymond Cirmo and his lovely wife, Julie, for their invaluable guidance, trust, and sincere advice, spurring me onward toward my goals.

My gratitude to Anna Caso for her loving care, loyalty, and constant friendship.

In loving memory and thankfulness to my mother, for instilling in me the importance of using wisdom to survive in this unpredictable world.

A special thank-you to the precious individuals and kind strangers who reached out to me with helping hands, caring words, and kind deeds along the way. And to the many readers of my column, "A New You," in newspapers across the country, whose heartwarming letters have inspired me. I am truly blessed and appreciative of you.

"For I have derived much joy and comfort
from your love." —Philemon 1:7.

"Every work that he began . . . he did it with all his heart, and prospered." —2 Chronicles 31:21.

Contents

PART TWO—BODY ❧ 87

PART THREE—SPIRIT ❧ 163

Introduction

This book you now hold in your hand can transform your life. Writing it transformed mine.

Within these pages are the secrets for a victorious life. Each is written with love, faith, and promise, out of tragedy and triumph from my hand to your heart. This is a formula of belief, which can turn defeat into victory and open the door to a wide terrain of possibilities.

I don't have to think that far back to the time in my life when I had almost nothing. Nothing except a 5" x 7" piece of faded white stationery that I had tucked away in the smooth, secret folds of my Bible. Written on that piece of paper was a detailed list of my innermost dreams, goals, and hopes for the future. That tattered paper became my companion as I traveled on the road of life.

Through the uphill climbs and winding paths, I learned how to bring my mind, body, and spirit into alignment, to link them together, to receive the power to excel, achieve my goals, persevere over extraordinary odds, and overcome every obstacle. The more connected you are with your mind, body, and spirit, the more you will enjoy the abundance of the universe and fulfill your wondrous desires.

At one time, all I had were dreams . . . and today when I read that list, my heart is filled with extreme gratitude, joy, and contentment. Each and every one of my heart's desires, written on that stationery so many years ago, has been granted. Seemingly impossible dreams have now come to pass.

And now, my dear readers, I want to share with you this special collection of writings, which can help you evolve into the most complete person that you can become. With these three components in order—the mind, body, and spirit—you can achieve tremendous success in all areas of your life.

This uplifting volume can recharge your whole being and restore the God-given flow within you for success. Then watch miracles begin to happen.

In each situation you encounter, ask yourself, "Is this good for my Mind? Body? Spirit?" If the answer is no, stop and get away from it right away.

Use the words in this life-renewing book as a guide to a better life. Read and reread, one page at a time, one day at a time, and incorporate these ideas into your own situations. Let this wisdom become a part of you as you discover good mental and physical health, peace of mind, and happiness.

Our journey through life cannot be made alone. We have been brought together for a very important reason. As I sit in my office, with the glorious sunlight streaming in from the picture window and my precious children happily playing in the front yard, I realize the immense joy I'm experiencing while preparing this for you. It feels as though God's hand is resting gently upon mine, so that as you read the words inscribed in this book, a divine transformation will take place in your life.

Hold my hand and let me be your friend, as I reveal to you the powerful messages within these heartfelt pages. Who knows what miraculous plans the Lord has in store for us?

Take my hand. I promise, it is not too late.

Catherine

2002

Part One

MIND

"The longer I live, the more I realize the impact of attitude on life. Attitude is more important than facts. It is more important than the past, education, than money, success, than what other people think or say or do. It is more important than appearance, giftedness or skill. It will make or break a company . . . a church . . . a home."

—*Charles Swindoll*

God Has a Plan for the Life of Every Person

The One who formed the brilliant stars and made the vast oceans created you out of His great love. His genuine devotion to His children lights the way as we travel through life.

God's love is sincere and constant and knows no boundaries or limits. Just as each star has its place and course, God has given to each of us a divine purpose, a plan for our lives.

As your guide, He will take you out of confusion and will help you to reach your destiny.

You are a worthwhile, significant, and valuable person. Since the beginning of time, there has never been anyone else exactly like you and there never will be again. You're capable of great things and deserve the best.

There is no one who can duplicate all of the attributes that only you possess. You are precious and are esteemed the most valuable treasure on earth. Generously equipped in both mind and body, you can do miraculous things with your life.

You have extraordinary capabilities and the world can benefit from your many talents. Utilize your full potential to make it a better place for yourself and for generations to follow. Everyone has many gifts to offer; find what you are best at and give that gift to others. A talent concealed or not expressed soon dries up and withers away, so extend it out to the world. It is like a little pebble that is dropped into the ocean, and the countless rings that are formed from its beginning are constantly getting bigger and bigger.

Have a healthy self-respect. God made you very special, so hold a high opinion of your own worth. Exude an air of gentle confidence.

People will perceive you as you perceive yourself.

Gentleness is not an absence of power, but a sign of great inner strength. How you act will determine how people will react to you.

Self-confidence differs from conceit or arrogance. It is a calm, serenely poised attitude that dares to achieve the very best.

Do not be afraid. Every noble acquisition has its risk. But you can adjust to any challenge or hardship if you have a desire to overcome. Shake off any mistakes of the day. God gives you new opportunities each morning.

This life is your constant opportunity. Create your own special dreams. Never be convinced that your goals are too high. Let others dig a cave; you can build a castle!

As a child of God, you, too, deserve the best; nothing is too good for you. Be what you dream to be and make your life everything you always hoped for.

You have complete control over the choices you make, so use wisdom. Choose respect, not ruthlessness. Make sure your choices will benefit not only yourself, but others as well, and your success will be sweet.

Do not listen to those who try to demean you. There will be some who will be jealous of you and who will try to distract you from your dreams.

Be strong. Never allow another person to rob you of doing your best to achieve your goals. Believe in yourself; I believe in you.

Just as each star is distinct and one of a kind, so are you. This life is your occasion to shine. So, give out your own radiant light, encouraging and inspiring others, while sharing joy and promise.

This is the dawning of a new day and "A New You."

Imagination Carries People over Mountains

Your possibilities reach as far as your eyes can see . . . and even farther.

Our imagination can carry us over mountains of obstacles . . . if used right.

We live in a world in which everything is possible. Forge ahead and reach beyond your goals. The resource of life is in the heart and the determination that comes from it.

By the glow of the lamp I write in my journal . . . and reminisce.

Every closed door I encountered, each "no" I received, every disappointment and trial—God meant it for good. If you persist, if you continue, if you try again and then again, you will be the victor. The prizes of life are not only in the beginning of your journey; they are also close to the end. Because you have lived longer and are much wiser, your prizes change, and the value of everyday treasures becomes greater. You have lived long enough to know that riches and society do not completely satisfy. But the hug of a little child, the whisper of prayer and thanksgiving, satisfies and lifts your soul to the heights.

Continue onward and upward, take one more step and you will find, as I have found, "Ask and it shall be given to you; seek and you shall find; knock and it shall be opened unto you."—Matthew 7:7.

We all have been blessed with many wonderful talents. It is the day of discovery, so begin now to permeate your life with love and give that treasure out to the world. Discover who you are. You are unique to God and have something very special to offer to others. Don't let anything dampen your spirit. Have confidence in your ability and capacity to achieve.

I once read about the awesome American portrait painter John

Singer Sargent. His critics, who faulted his work for making his subjects seem more beautiful than the critics thought they were, praised one of his smaller works, a painting of a panel of roses.

Sargent was offered great sums of money for this piece, but he refused to sell it. Why? Because whenever the artist was discouraged or doubtful of his abilities, he would look at his painting and say to himself, "I painted this." His confidence would then return. Sargent became the chosen portrait artist of presidents' wives and the wealthy and famous.

People will criticize you, so you might as well decide what you want to be criticized about. Others will laugh and scorn you, but ignore them, while your love projects and brings about your desired goal.

This is your life. Why settle for the mediocre? Why just follow the crowd? A life filled with love and appreciation is the only life worth living.

Be prepared to work hard at it. There is no easy ride to the throne. A poet wrote, "Must I be carried to heaven on a flowery bed of ease? While others fought to win the prize and sailed on bloody seas." Turn defeats into victories by much prayer, humbleness, and patience. You can control your attitude toward circumstances. Choose the word "will" over "won't."

It is never too late to become someone great in God's eyes. But the way up is down—down on your knees. Present your heart's desire to Him and consider your motivation, attitude, and objective. Ask God to let His gift, which He put in you, be expressed to its fullest and highest.

Dare to look toward triumph; set forth to achieve it today. Remember, there is only one thing we take out of this world: our character. And what we have become in that realm determines our value here and our destination there.

Feed the White Dog That Lives Inside of You

An old Indian chief once said to a young preacher, "Ever since I have given my heart to God, I find that within me there is a fight between the black dog and the white dog." Listening in amazement, the preacher asked, "Chief, which one wins?" The wise old chief remained silent for quite a few moments, then gave a very profound answer: "The one that I feed the most."

Each day we pray for strength and wisdom to do our best. What you will be next week is what you have said or done today. The power that will be the strongest tomorrow is the one you have fed this day.

What do you and your family watch on television? What are the words to the music you are listening to? Does it promote violence and hate or peace and love?

To be happy you must grasp with open arms all the loveliness of the world. God has shown you what He likes in His beautiful creation and has painted a masterpiece for you to see. Notice the lovely dappled pattern on the road, made by sunlight filtering through the leaves. After a rainfall, witness the multitude of colors in the magnificent rainbow.

What thoughts do you play over and over again in your mind? It is universally known that what you think, you will become. We must strive for peace, joy, and contentment, food for the right mental attitude. Our thoughts are the basic foundation of our character, our happiness, successes, or failures. Thoughts produce feelings, positive or negative, and feelings control our action or inaction.

A very simple child's story holds the proven key to every success. The little engine said over and over and over again, "I think I can. I think I can. I think I can." And guess what? He could. In order to think "we can," we have to feed positive images into our mind, actual pictures of every single step of our success.

If you use your imagination to worry, change it to picture the successful outcome of every problem. If you use your memory to remember your hurts and failures, change it to remember the sweet and beautiful things of your life.

Feed the white dog with powerful truths. Stock the pantry of your heart with life-giving food from the Bible, the wisdom of sages, inspirational poetry, and even the advice of a trusted friend.

A definite time set aside at the beginning of each day to give thanks and to ask for guidance to the open door of God's will is the key to ultimate victory.

During your day, help someone in some small way, once in the morning and again in the afternoon. Brighten their day with a deliberate act of courtesy, a short note, a token of generosity, or a few reassuring words.

Good deeds will return in a miraculous way to create in you that Supreme Love that never fails, for these are God's acts and His ways.

At the end of the day, the last thing left in the subconscious feeds the soul all through the night. Let it be an act of putting into God's care any unsolved problem, for with the dawn's light will come the solution.

I love Philippians 4, which encourages us to think this way: "Whatsoever things are true, whatsoever things are honest, whatsoever things are just, whatsoever things are pure, whatsoever things are lovely, whatsoever things are of good report: If there be any virtue [strength] or any praise [happiness] you must think on these things."

That is a law written in the Word of God, a law as positive and proven as the law of gravity. A law to bring you happiness and strength, so that when battles come, you will be fortified . . . and strengthened to always be the victor.

Put the Needs of Others Before Your Own

The six most important words are "Forgive me Lord, I was wrong." The five most important words are "I'm so glad I'm forgiven." The four most important words are "Keep on, keeping on." The three most important words are "I love you." The two most important words are "Thank you." The least important word is "Mine."

How important are our words, our speech, and our daily conversations? Your words can make you or break you. Choose them wisely and let them be simple phrases full of humility, for only the humble can truly learn. "Humble yourselves therefore under the mighty hand of God, that He may exalt you in due time."—1 Peter 5:6.

Practice makes perfect, so begin to exercise your freedom to change your mind and be transformed. Admitting that you are wrong turns failure to success, confusion to peace. Realizing you are forgiven gives you freedom to carry on and opens the door to creative energy and joy.

So many people hold grudges their whole life. They don't forgive and forget. They don't realize that if one buries the hatchet, one shouldn't leave the handle sticking out.

When all the hang-ups are gone, we are free to pursue our dreams and goals, prayerfully persisting onward. In our dealings with mankind, our motivation must be divine love. This comes only by yielding yourself through God. It is He who will love through you, and in expressing it genuinely, we become undefeatable.

Saying "thank you" is next to saying "I love and appreciate you." This restores harmony and clears the way for greater achievement.

Let us forget the small world of self. We must not live in the realm of "me" or "mine," coveting all for our own satisfaction, for that kind of satisfaction never really remains.

I once heard a powerful story of a man who was escorted by an angel down into hell. There, the man saw a round table with a big bowl of delicious food in the middle of it. Sitting around the table were people who were holding three-foot-long spoons in their hands. They were wretched, skeletal, and starving, because the spoons were long enough to reach the food, but too long to put the food in their mouths. In anger and frustration, they tried desperately to feed themselves.

The man turned his back on their torment, shaking his head. Then, the angel escorted him up to heaven.

There, he saw an identical table and the mouthwatering bowl of food in the center. Again, there were three-foot-long golden spoons. But the people around the table were glowing with health and joy, and dazzling light, laughter, and song filled the room. And in great love, they were feeding each other.

This is the only secret to true happiness and what our Lord came to show us: "Love your neighbor as much as you love and care for yourself and do to others what you would have them do to you." Doing kind deeds for others and extending a warm, loving hand will be a lasting joy.

It is so happy to love. Look around you and treat yourself to the greatest joy in life, which is doing some little thing for someone else and saying, "God told me to do this for you." Precious readers, I extend my golden spoon out to you today, filled with the honey of God's love and wisdom that He has fed my heart. It is my great joy to know it will fill you with the secret of the only true success in life.

An Attitude of Gratitude
Sees You Through

The Good Lord sometimes allows me to have a disturbing dream in the night to adjust my attitude, to show me what could be and to help me appreciate all the good things and blessings that I have. For the enemy tries to make me dissatisfied with the status of my life, as he does to us all.

When in the morning I awake to calm, to knowing that everything really is all right, I know that the Lord has given me the greatest lesson of all—appreciation for the design by which He has shaped my life so far. When I start thanking Him for every good thing, then I literally do wake up.

Living your life with gratitude is the only way to have the right attitude to carry you through day after day.

Yes, we are so busy—we have careers, families, and homes to take care of. Yes, there are people who try to get you down, but there are others whose friendship is so valuable and precious. Yes, we have heartaches and trials, but we also have blessings and joys beyond measure. Sometimes, you just have to look for them and focus on them. Focus is really just another word for discipline.

If we leave our mind unguarded, then the enemy can put every kind of negative thought into it. It is his job to make us dissatisfied with everything God has given us and every person He has put in our lives. But I believe every one of us is smart enough to know his tactics and to know how to defeat his darts. "Do not be overcome by evil, but overcome evil with good."—Romans 12:21.

We must first look on all human beings with eyes of compassion. This was one of Jesus' greatest attributes. He showed us that the quality of a compassionate person is a beautiful one. Isn't it wonderful to read an essay that states with understanding just what you have been going through? Compassion and understanding, filled with love, is healing.

When you wake up in the morning you have to smile. You have twenty-four brand-new hours before you. God gave this present to you. It's only polite to say thank you to someone who gives you a gift. Vow to live each hour full of purpose and gratefulness, every waking moment, and the strength of His love will flow into your life.

Be determined to have the right attitude, the attitude of gratitude. God forgives and overlooks all kinds of failures if our attitude to Him is of love, thankfulness, and determination to do better each and every day.

Behold the beauty and wonder that surrounds you. Lift the shades of your mind and let the Son shine in. You can view the beautiful outdoors and listen closely to the sounds of nature, the trees rustling, the birds chirping.

We have to pull together to get up this road in life. And there are definite directions to reach our destination. At the end of each day give yourself time to read the directions that tell you how to get to that lovely celestial city written of in the Bible. And talk with the Map Maker to be sure you understand every hidden turn.

I am writing to tell you, dear readers, of the challenges I encounter every day, and I'm giving you my secrets of how to overcome your challenges and reach your destination with joy and rejoicing.

Be Glad Every Day

What color are you going to paint your world? It is up to you. Dip the paintbrush of your life in the glory of the rainbow colors, where joy and beauty reign. You are one of a special kind, a unique creation of God. Bask in the glowing light of His love.

One evening, while watching the movie classic *Pollyanna*, the touching story about a little girl whose parents were killed while serving as missionaries, one statement stayed with me. Pollyanna spoke of a quote from Abraham Lincoln that she wore around her neck in a locket that her father had given to her. It read, "When you look for the bad in mankind expecting to find it, you surely will."

Then, Pollyanna went on to say, "After my father heard that quote, he looked only for the good in people and made up the 'glad game.'" This was a game her father started to cover up the disappointments of a life of poverty, as the only clothes they had were to be found in the barrels of charity sent to Africa from America.

Then, Pollyanna went on to recall her father saying, "If God took the trouble to tell us in the Bible eight hundred times to be glad and happy, He must have wanted us to do it." And I agree! We all have had our share of disappointments in life, and we must have a regimen of discipline to combat the negativity that bombards our minds.

So we want to saturate our whole being with, as Pollyanna said, the "glad" verses in the Bible. Let's put them in our memory and repeat them in our minds and speak them aloud from our mouths each day. I will start your list for you and let you complete the treasures:

"He was anointed with the oil of gladness above all His fellows."—Psalm 45:7.
"Thou has put gladness in my heart."—Psalm 126:5.

"Light is sown for the righteous and gladness for the upright in heart."—Psalm 97:11.

"This is the day that the Lord has made, I will rejoice and be glad in it."—Psalm 118:24.

"But let the righteous be glad; let them rejoice before God; yea, let them exceedingly rejoice."—Psalm 68:3.

"Come before His presence with thanksgiving and make a joyful noise unto the Lord."—Psalm 95:2.

"In the multitude of my thoughts within me, thy comforts delight my soul."—Psalm 94:19.

"The Lord is my defense and my God is the rock of my refuge."—Psalm 94:22.

According to the American Heritage Dictionary, the word "glad" means "feeling, showing or giving joy and pleasure; happy; pleased, willing." Gladness of heart is a beautiful quality. It is a celebration of life and one can see it in a person's actions, words, and deeds.

We live in a world that can communicate every disaster that happens on earth. That can be a tactic of the enemy. His one purpose is to destroy everything that is good, honest, and beautiful.

I take my burdens to the Lord and thank Him for the great privilege of knowing Him. I trust in God's unconditional love and wait in patience and faith. I'm speaking from my own experience, and I can assure you that God is faithful and the enemy will not triumph over you.

Look for the best in others, behold and rejoice in the bud of promise in people, and bring it out in full bloom. Then, in the evening of your life, you can hold in your arms a vast bouquet of those whose lives give forth a sweet perfume in response to your love.

Watch and see how your world will change as you live a life of thanksgiving, adding a "glad" verse to your memory each day. And so surround yourself with gladness. Choose to be glad and rejoice in it!

Let the Mountains Echo with God's Love

High on the majestic mountaintop in the beauty of a clear blue sky, with the sun shining brightly and the wind blowing briskly, voices were heard.

"Hello-o-o-o," a young mountain climber shouted. And in the distance a voice answered, "Hello-o-o-o." The novice climber looked around; there was no one in sight.

Again he called, "Hello-o-o-o, who are you?" Seconds later the voice said, "Hello-o-o-o, who are you?" And then one more time, he said, "I'm John Doe-o-o-o."

And the voice answered, "I'm John Doe-o-o-o." It was at that moment that the young mountain climber knew that the voice he heard was his own echo.

Your life becomes an echo as the years pass. It eventually gives back everything that you say, your deeds and your attitude. It returns to you that which you yourself create. That is why we must seriously consider the long-range consequences of our actions. The thoughts of your mind determine the spontaneous words of your mouth.

In all aspects of your life, remember the echo. A joy-filled, obedient, and thankful heart is the best service we can give to God. He knows in doing so we show our confidence in His love. He is our Creator, our Father, so have confidence in your abilities. We each have special attributes that are ours alone, given to us by Him. One person can make a difference. Look at Thomas Edison, who brought light into so many lives.

You are "one" and can change your world. Be curious; ask questions. Knowledge is powerful and something you must acquire. "There is gold and a multitude of rubies but the lips of wisdom are worth more than precious jewels."—Proverbs 20:15.

Success does not lie in public acclaim but in becoming the best at what you do.

To work for the common good of mankind is the greatest of all service. We are here on earth to make it a better place. Create your echo. If you want more love in your life, give more love. If you desire joy, then persist in being thankful and make it happen.

We all have trials; if it's not one thing it's another. When I am in the midst of hard times and the forces of evil seem to be against me, I remember that the Bible says, "In everything give Him thanks for He will work it together for your good." Remember also, "Vengeance is mine, I will repay, says the Lord," and "The wheels of God grind slowly but grind on."

Give it up to Him. We don't want bitterness and resentment to be our echo as life goes on. Many struggle with bitterness, but know that if you give it to the Lord, He will work things out for His good. Although we cannot change people, we can change ourselves.

Keep trying and eventually you will succeed, for I know that St. Paul confirms the "echo response" in the Bible: "In due season, we will reap if we faint not."

So let us shout joy, love, and exultant bravery from our mountaintops. Give out to others words of encouragement, strength, compassion, and understanding, rejoicing in their achievements, sharing laughter in the joy of life. And the rooftops, the hills, and the mountains will echo back continually, "Your life is full of joy," "You are of great value," "You have been faithful," "You will make it because you have trusted in God to bring it to pass according to His promise."

Let your life sing, "He taught me how to watch and pray and go rejoicing every day, oh, happy day, oh, happy day!"

You Deserve Everything Wonderful

I showed him the 3" x 5" sticky note that I saved and carried with me for the past nine years. At that particular time I was having a very challenging day when this special friend wrote a simple sentence on the paper. He handed it to me and said, "For you only." Reading it later and alone, I knew I would always cherish it.

When I was sad, I'd look at the little note and be lifted up. If I felt alone, I'd read it and be comforted; and when I was made to feel inferior, it would remind me of my worth.

Now, years later, his face lit up with surprise as I took out the very faded pink note that read, "You are wonderful and are worth every good thing that happens to you."

"Those kind and caring words got me through so many hard times," I said. "Thank you, my friend."

Compassion, kind advice, and counsel can help to transform a person's life for the better. Matthew 25:40 says, "In as much as you have done it to the least of my brothers, you have done it to me." Just think, your kind words and deeds are noted by God.

Reaching for cherished dreams can be difficult and depressing, with many stumbling blocks along the way. But you can achieve your heart's desire by always acknowledging His ways to encourage another, to influence positively.

When you plant kindness, you harvest love. See God manifested through you by daily exercise. I have a friend who has a plaque on her kitchen wall that reads, "There is no better exercise for the heart than to reach down and lift up another."

I know the Bible says, "It is more blessed to give than to receive."

And blessed means happy. So be full of joy all year long by sharing, caring, and giving to others. The best time to give is when someone least expects it; then the surprise of joy is never forgotten.

A resident of Venice, Florida, wrote, "Giving is much more than buying a gift. Take a moment to call or send a cheery card to a friend or a patient in the hospital. Focus on things that make other people smile and talk of happy memories. Mostly just tell them that you love them." Accompany that with a hug!

The best present you can receive is a true friend. Friends give in ways that only the heart can see and are a shoulder of support when you need it the most. Friends are always there to lean on and their smiles warm the coldest day. They encourage you to do the seemingly impossible and they delight in your accomplishments. Build up the confidence and self-esteem of others by telling them they are one of a kind. Let them know they are worthy, special, and precious in God's sight. Be generous with compliments and praise.

Insults, rude remarks, and sarcasm can take their toll on even the strongest individual. Never allow anyone's hurtful actions or negative comments to keep you from being your very best. Just resolve right now to devote your time and energy to pursuing your own special dreams. Of course this won't make you popular with the "crowd," but your life is much too valuable to waste one single moment. There are mountains to climb and glorious heights above and beyond the gloom of spiteful people.

You are a precious gift from God and need to grow in the sunshine of His love. As someone who cares, you are able to express your love in a unique way. The world needs you, God needs you, and I want you to know, dear readers, from my heart to yours, that you are wonderful and deserve everything good that happens to you.

Remain Calm and Happiness Will Follow

Confederate General Stonewall Jackson once said, "Let me tell you a way to happiness . . . it is to be calm in every situation."

There is much wisdom to be found in those simple words. To be calm, at peace and contented, surely is one of the secrets to true happiness.

In times of calmness and tranquility we have a chance to rest; to evaluate our lives and gain valuable insight; to appreciate our well-being, our dreams, and the unlimited possibilities for the future; and to realize a higher purpose in our lives.

The word "calm" is defined as "not agitated or tumultuous. Quiet, serene, absence of emotional turmoil, serenity." Life has a way of working out when we become aware of this pattern and have the revelation that is needed to just wait in quiet faith.

I once read about a wise lady who drew what she called her "worry chart." In this chart she kept a record of the things that distressed her. After a period of time her discovery was that most of the things she worried about probably would never happen.

A small percentage of her concerns were about past decisions that she could not rectify, and some of her anxiety was about other people's criticisms. Her study concluded that only 5 percent of her worries were legitimate. So take note of this, and do not let worry inhibit your happiness.

Happy people make the best of every situation because happiness is all in your attitude. Be optimistic about the future. Studies show that positive thoughts and behavior have a positive impact on the biochemistry of the brain, raising levels of serotonin, the neurotransmitter linked with feelings of happiness.

Laughter produces a relaxation response. If you can laugh at your mistakes and keep on persisting, you will eventually find success. Mark Twain said, "The human race has one really effective weapon and that is laughter." Practice good humor to keep you calm in trying situations. Humor can help to make the rough ways smooth. Try to find the amusing side of every situation.

Let your interests be as wide as possible and let your reaction to things and persons that interact with you be friendly, rather than hostile.

Nurture close relationships. Those who have a backup support system tend to be less stressed and cope better.

Life can be difficult, so focus your thoughts on solving any problems you may have, and assume you will overcome. "The things that hurt instruct," said Benjamin Franklin. True character is exhibited in a crisis. Hold steady in your heart to gain beauty of character in every difficulty.

Be thankful for whatever you are able to do. It is easy to take for granted a gift that we have been born with. But we are here to find out that the secret to how happily we can live lies in the ability of how freely we give.

Give out a little bit of your joy each day and watch it multiply within you. Simple pleasures will become major delights. Take charge of your time. Become conscious of how you're spending your day. Don't waste it.

Cultivate your spiritual being. Faith gives life a higher meaning, and you can lose yourself in the joy of doing what God created you to do.

Of all that I have written and for all that we have learned together, know that the wisest of all persons is the one who seeks God . . . and the most successful one of all is the person who has found God. May you be blessed today with the secret of happiness.

Keep Your Eye on Your Goals and Forge Ahead

A Chinese proverb tells us, "With time and patience the mulberry leaf becomes a silk gown." In patience is the power to be transformed. Employ it and luxuriate in the resulting success.

No matter what we personally want, we have to pay the price with our time. Working hard consistently over a long period will almost guarantee triumph. Whether you are starting a company, managing a business, caring for the home, or running the country, there is no shortcut to being the best. It takes self-sacrifice, devotion, and hard work to be successful.

The first step to getting what you want out of life is to decide what you want. Work hard, but make sure you love the work. You must keep in mind that the menial work of the beginning is just a step to your wonderful goal. Be patient enough to stick with your goal until it comes to fruition. Passion and planning equal success.

Be a person of honesty and integrity. The greatest rewards begin when we change our thinking from "What's in it for me?" to "How can I help you?" The more you help others succeed, the more that you will be a success in your heart.

Patience is a virtue, a strength. It is an essential key to achievement, but without perseverance, it won't happen. Remember the saying "Where there's a will there's a way." Set your will on "persevere" and leave it there.

Do not let the negative opinions of others stop you from pursuing your dreams. Be determined to forge ahead. Follow your heart; it will lead you to the place you want to go.

Aristotle said, "Criticism is something we can avoid easily by saying nothing, doing nothing, and being nothing." It is a fact that people develop at different rates. Albert Einstein was seven years old before he could read, didn't speak until he was four, and flunked math. Isaac Newton did poorly in grade school. An editor of a newspaper fired Walt Disney for lack of ideas. So much for criticism!

Success takes stamina, stability, courage, and a desire to learn from others. Go to the library and read the biographies of successful people. Copy their style of perseverance and apply it to your own unique ideas. You will realize soon enough that those who made it just never gave up. Perseverance gives power to weakness and opens the doors to closed dreams. No matter how difficult things appear to be, do not ever give up on your heart's plans. Believe in your own worth and make those plans surpass your highest hopes.

Success is measured differently, and that depends on your own personal goal. Some people gauge success in dollars and cents; others measure it in love. A great goal of some is to gain success by triumphing over emotional obstacles. Whatever success is to you, you will know when it begins to happen.

Sometimes, I think, our perception of success changes with time. My dreams as a little girl of being a ballerina and beauty queen have been accomplished, but my gauge of success changed when I realized that the joy of my life is to be in God's presence and to help others—to encourage, enlighten, and comfort as I have been encouraged, enlightened, and comforted.

It is wonderful to redefine our concept of success, to change, to grow in wisdom and maturity. May God bless you and give you your heart's desire. That's what makes life so exciting . . . that with God's help, every day is a new beginning as you become "A New You."

Kind Words Can Work Miracles

I once read a story about a small boy who had a bad temper. The boy's father gave him a hammer and a bag of nails and told his son, "Every time you lose your temper, hammer a nail into the fence." During the weeks that followed, the young boy learned to control his temper, and the number of times he hammered nails dwindled.

Soon, the boy didn't lose his temper at all. "Next," said the father, "for each day you are able to control your anger, pull one nail out of the fence." After about a month, the young boy finally told his father that all the nails were out of the fence. The father and son walked hand in hand to the fence and the father said, "You have done well. But look at the holes in the fence; it will never be the same. When you say things in anger, they will leave a scar just like these holes."

If you wound someone by a verbal abuse, it can be as bad as a physical one. So let us fill up those holes with loving words and kind deeds until the holes will be forgotten. By God's grace we can take control of every situation and turn life around. We can create the right atmosphere by saying the right thing.

No matter how old we get, kind and encouraging words, when spoken from the heart at the precise moment, can achieve miracles. Words of understanding and compassion are the gateways between worry and peace. They are like showers of blessings to the recipient.

Sometimes taking control means not saying anything. Silence is a form of understanding. Listening to a person's words can help them sort out their problems. We should listen to our own words sometimes. Have you ever made a statement and then quickly said, "No, I didn't really mean that," because you suddenly heard your statement aloud and knew it came out sounding childish or overreactive. Then, a smile of under-standing made you speak genuinely and kindly to others. Having sincere consideration of their feelings provides the bedding ground for God to bring to life the seeds of great wisdom.

Vow to speak only words that will build up another. It will do won-ders for someone's attitude, productivity, and creativity. Praise people sin-cerely. Don't save up compliments; unspoken, they go to waste. Tell others what they did that was valuable, outstanding, or helpful, and how good their words or deeds made you feel. Don't hesitate to encourage people to repeat a good performance. More than likely, if you praise them, they will want to continue their good efforts.

Give a hug or a pat on the back when appropriate. Life is measured by the words we say, the cheer we spread, the things we do, and the way we do them. By blessing others, blessings will return to you.

True kindness and caring touches can turn sorrow into the sweet-ness that brings us closer to God, to experience all the great depths of the wisdom and joy of life.

And so today, dear readers, begin to take control of your life. Start with prayer to the One who has complete control over the ultimate destination of each one of us, as we make the daily choices of our actions and words.

The Tiny Ant Offers a Huge Inspiration

*T*oday we will learn one of the greatest secrets of success from a tiny ant.

There is no royal road over which we are carried to achieve anything noteworthy, one step at a time and each step in succession. That which steadily perseveres will endure.

I know the Book of Proverbs says, "Go watch the ant, you who are not trying hard enough."

There was once a soldier who was forced to hide from his enemies in an abandoned cement silo. He had been on the run for days. Exhausted and weary, he almost gave in to hopelessness. As the soldier looked down on the barren floor, there appeared a tiny ant. The insect was carrying a crumb of bread and was attempting to climb up the high, steep wall. The crumb kept falling, but the ant refused to give up.

The man counted the ant's attempts to get the crumb up to a window to the outside. The crumb fell seventy times to the ground. The soldier watched in awe as each time the ant again and again patiently shouldered its burden and continued to try. The ant persevered. On the seventy-first time the insect reached the top. That tiny ant's persistence gave the man courage and hope to keep on trying. Two days later, he was free.

God sent His grace with a great example of encouragement in the form of a tiny ant. If you think nothing of importance is happening around you, then perhaps you are being too careless in your observation. Observe everything and everybody. And remember the saying, "Practice makes perfect."

Everyone has a reason for being here. If you have breath in your body, you have a goal yet to achieve. The best goal God recognizes is the goal you have that will help and uplift someone else. Persist to make the world a better place. You can do it. There is a way to make a difference. God blesses those who keep on trying. There must be something you can do for someone else. You can make your goal a certain number of smiles to give each day. If you give, you will automatically receive. So give help, encouragement, and the joy of life to others.

If you want to write a book that you feel will help others, don't give up. If you want to paint a picture to give others insight to beauty, never quit. If you want to give your own family more joy, continue to persist.

Make something extraordinary out of your life. First your task will seem impossible. Then, it will be difficult. Finally, with persistence, it will get done!

If you only knew the love that God has for you and how beautiful you are in His sight, you would never be discouraged again. Pray to see yourself through His eyes, and you will be amazed at how much more beautiful you become each day. God can reveal to you your true potential. You have so much talent and the ability to do anything! Just never give up! He made each person to accomplish something great. You were born with a great capacity for giving. All you need is a compassionate, caring heart committed to God, and He will direct your path.

Even through adversity, keep on trying. God is with the person who refuses to quit. Eventually you will reach your destiny. So start today.

Ask God, "What can I do?" Get one of those bracelets with "W.W.J.D." on it and ask yourself daily, "What Would Jesus Do?" Somehow, you will begin to know what you are supposed to do to shed life, love, and joy on the lives of others. You can do wonders. God placed a great ability for achievement in you. Just keep on, keeping on, and you will reach your goal with sure success!

Follow the Maestro's Lead and Arise

Arturo Toscanini was a cello player in a small European orchestra. He was nearsighted and couldn't see the music on the stand in front of him, so patiently and persistently he memorized it.

One evening, the orchestra's leader was unable to conduct. Toscanini stepped in to replace him, since he was the only orchestra member who knew the program. His performance was executed with perfection, and Toscanini became one of the finest conductors in the world. He turned a disadvantage into a blessing by going one step further than the norm. An unexpected turn became the path to success.

Truly dedicated people believe that unforeseen roadblocks cannot defeat them, because they are filled with a joy that tells them all things work together for good and that all things are possible for those who believe.

If you feel rejected or discouraged, when "no" seems to be the answer everywhere you turn, and circumstances seem against you, that is the time to regroup, reassess, and regenerate.

It was one of those days when I was at a standstill. As I searched for answers as to why I didn't seem to get anywhere, I turned randomly in the Bible to Acts 22:10. It stated, "And I said, What shall I do Lord? And the Lord said unto me, arise."

Shake off the lethargy and do something, anything, get up, begin, aspire, soar, proceed . . . arise. I grabbed the dictionary; Webster's defines arise as "to get up, to move upward." Success comes by going after and grasping your goals, not just sitting by and waiting. Persisting and pursuing time and time again—not giving in or giving up!

Then I turned to Ephesians 3:20, which confirmed, "Now unto him that is able to do exceedingly abundantly above all that we ask or think according to the power that works in us."

We are the hands, the feet, and the head. So we must realize that there is a plan, a divine purpose for every closed door, each rejection, and every "no." If we dare to persist, we will win and the victor's crown will be ours.

Tap into the ocean of God's creativity; your heart will become inspired and miracles will take place.

A St. Louis, Missouri, resident wrote via e-mail, "I am a business owner who believes my business is a blessing from God. I try to remain focused on Him daily, constantly believing He will make everything all right. Sometimes I have many customers and sometimes I have few, but I praise Him with all my heart and ask that He helps me remain patient and prayerful at all times, never taking my mind off Him."

That right attitude, coupled with all the creative ideas that God gives, can't help but lead to success!

The fine line where the azure of the sky gently touches the vast blue ocean, where the horizon becomes hazy, is the place where heaven touches earth. Don't forget, God's plan for your life is glorious.

God is fair to all. He will bless your faith, which cannot help but lead to good works. So whatever you desire to achieve for yourself, family, or others . . . have faith. When your faith and deeds together reach the same dedicated heights as Toscanini's, the greatness of your purpose in life will be revealed.

Every individual must play out the symphony of their own life, and when the lights dim, the murmuring audience quiets down, you must turn your eyes upon the heavenly conductor, God, . . . and begin.

You Start with a Calm and Clear Mind

You are walking on a diamond-littered snowy path. The beauty of God is all around you: the ruby colors of a cardinal hidden in the evergreens, icicles clinging to bare branches like a glittering necklace, the music of the stars, and the vast canvas of the sky—a masterpiece.

Now among all this glory, beauty, and majesty, are you going to start thinking negative thoughts?

I read in Proverbs 23:7, "For as he thinketh in his heart, so he is." Thoughts are strengthening and life-giving. When the mind is calm and clear, how quickly and how smoothly you will perceive everything. Things that once were mundane are now so beautiful. Be silent for a moment; go within, where your soul can be quiet and tranquil. When the mind becomes still, you can really savor life.

To have peace, harmony, and vitality, you must keep your mind on the positives.

When God is enthroned in our hearts, we listen and follow where He leads. God is called "the comforter," "the counselor." His spirit brings us understanding and consoles us. We never walk alone in this world; He is the only source of everlasting love, joy, and peace.

I've seen it time and time again . . . the power of positive thinking. It's not just a magic formula, not just any old thought; the power lies in what you choose to think on. In the Bible there is a world of wisdom and a solution to every known problem. If you ask God to reveal those of His words that will create your victory and then search through the Scriptures, you will find them.

Thinking positive thoughts can transform a life. So much depends on how you view situations that are presented to you. The enemy can wreak havoc on your mind, but the conqueror must advance boldly. The mind is the battleground. Your thinking can make you or break you.

Can you imagine the disastrous consequences of bringing up a child without any training whatsoever? Toddlers automatically pick up anything they see and put it in their mouths or throw it on the floor. They need to be potty-trained and need to know not to touch hot stoves and fire.

I know the Bible says a child comes into the world with a nature that lies automatically, hence the great need for training. Do you think we can leave our mind untrained? If we do, we are in for it! Do you discipline your mind? I do. I must. It is our duty to ourselves and to others, for as a man thinks in his heart, so is he.

Ask God for a transformation in your life. I read in Job 23:11, "My foot has held His steps and not declined to walk in them." This means to think on God's ways and do them.

Remember that our mind is the battleground, and God has allowed the enemy free access to ravage it . . . but only if we allow him. God wants us to develop character, so we must post the word of God at the entrance of our minds. As a mighty angel who repels every defeating thought, we must be faithful to ourselves and keep our arsenal full of His promises.

There is a word of life and victory for every situation. We are conquerors, so let's walk in heavenly places, far above all negative principalities and powers. This is our privilege and the highest form of worship to God. Thinking His thoughts makes us become like Him.

Know that we have the knowledge and that it is up to us to take it, live it . . . and be a mighty conqueror. There is no other way to be victorious.

Precious Thoughts Spring from the Children

How my little girls are growing. Day by day we see changes that we marvel at. I look over my shoulder and see their individual characters materializing before me.

How proud we are when our children accomplish difficult tasks, with their expanding vocabulary and manual dexterity and awareness of love. God's most beautiful thoughts bloom in our children and give our love life by a greater awareness of His love.

But watching them grow up so quickly saddens me, too. How fast time passes. A part of me wants them to stay small forever: holding a scratched tiny finger out and saying "Boo, boo" and wanting me to kiss the hurt away. Running into my arms after a tumble. Their small hands tightly holding ours as we cross the street. How humbling these precious moments are. And how much I am enjoying these priceless years.

As a parent, mentor, friend, or sibling, you are a person of influence. God has a great purpose for you: to impart values, strengths, and wisdom, to stimulate creativity, and to help bring forth gifts that God has placed into an individual's life.

You are expanding another's world with words, imagination, humor, and strength-giving thoughts. Parents and caregivers can teach children to really "see," to enrich their life with beauty, train them to exercise control, and stimulate their intellect with exposure to great music, literature, and arts.

Encourage children to read the Word of God. It will personally meet their deepest need. Don't rely on the television to entertain your children, for you have no control on what will flash before them. Have focused attention on what goes into their ears and what is observed by their eyes.

Teach them how to see what is good, and train them to hear what is right. Tenderly extend your time to children and develop their own unique strengths and individual personalities.

Many adults say it was at "their parent's knee" that they gained their earliest inspiration. Be kinder in your tone of voice, in your choice of words, and in your touch. God has given into your hands His most priceless treasures and has given us an assignment to unveil and keep in perfect condition this work of art. Child rearing is increasingly complex, so pray every day that God will lead you to say the right things, to speak the truth in love.

Your loving leadership will guide them to achieving great success in life, whether that is as a homemaker, a mechanic, a waitress, a doctor. It will teach them that serving others is a position of honor, for God said, "What so ever you have done to the least of these, my little ones, you have done for me." And you will find that raising a child is not a one-way occupation, for they will return unto you a fresh awareness of all creation.

"We find delight in the beauty and happiness of children that makes the heart too big for the body."—Ralph Waldo Emerson.

Make your number-one priority turning their hearts and their minds to God, last thing at night and first thing in the morning, and creating in them at every meal the expression of a thankful and happy heart. A family in the Lord will always get closer together.

Read Bible stories with them. Use God's Word to give understanding to the solution of ordinary problems that we face every day. This will make a lasting impact on their lives. Seeking His wisdom daily should be a priority for all those who nurture children.

Before mealtime, if my husband and I forget to pray, we glance over at our two-year-old daughter. With her tiny hands folded, eyes shining, she waits . . . and we look at each other and humbly bow our heads in thanksgiving that our little angel has brought us to the awareness of what is most important in life.

Resolve to Rise Above and Give Thanks

*T*here is a truth that we must be aware of, a power that works in our lives and a source of strength that we can tap into. We have all the resources needed to rise above any circumstance.

God has given us life's instruction book, the Bible, and an angel to watch over us. But the great question is, will we humble ourselves to be completely honest and submit to the Bible's commandments? (Commandments, not suggestions.) The Word of God will bring about the desired results if we choose to do it.

What's your basic attitude? Life is like a mirror: If you frown at it, it will frown back; if you smile, it returns the greeting. The decisions of the mind are very private, but the whole world sees the results.

Sometimes, our minds are like turbulent water, filled with confusion, regret, critical thoughts, and worry. When it rains, clean and pure water falls from the sky. Then, it picks up chemicals in the air, falls to the ground, and into the soil. The water is filtered as it flows through treatment plants, then purified by chlorine. By the time it reaches our faucet, it's as close as it can get to being as clean as it was the day it fell from the heavens.

Our minds are flooded daily by the ways of the world and all its bad news. We can purify our thoughts and make our paths straight if the Bible is our filter. It is invigorating and encouraging to know that by reading it, we can gain wisdom to make the right choices and get rid of the wrong. Ask yourself, can I do something about it? If so, do it. If not, give it to God and leave it there.

Today, dear readers, I am giving you a test. Let's find out what you really like. God teaches us by the law of contrasts. Which of these two seem best to you?

- When you wake up in the morning, would you rather groan about the job you go to or look up and say, "Thank you, Heavenly Father, that I have a job to help support my family," and then take that thankful attitude with you to work each day?
- Would you rather gripe to your coworkers that your client is stingy or say with a smile, "We're going to serve that client so well, it will bring us ten more" (and it will).
- When you come home from work, would you rather say hurtful words, causing a child to cry? Or sit on the floor and feel little arms around you, baby kisses on your cheek spreading rays of sunshine and laughter?
- Before dinner, do you want to sit down to the news of every tragedy and evil in the world? Or begin your meal with a prayer of thankfulness, asking God to bless your family and the food that you eat?
- Do you want to have a yelling match with your mate or a calm conversation in sincerity, accompanied with a smile of confidence that life's problems can be worked out with a hug of strength-giving love?
- At the end of the day, would you rather watch a violent movie or listen to serene music while reading encouraging words?

You can choose and change from what is making you unhappy to the things that will make you happy. I know that many of you grew up in homes and in situations that were less than perfect, to say the least. But we've all heard about many individuals who overcame such adversity. They lifted their minds, bodies, and spirits out of that horrible past and moved on to a successful future.

Choose this day whom you shall serve. For the one you yield your mind, voice, and muscles to is the one you have chosen to serve. As for me and my house, we will serve the Lord.

Persistence Helps Us Get Second Chances

There is something so wonderful about being given a "second chance," an opportunity to start again, to begin fresh and anew with a clean slate. An exciting new adventure to once again try to tackle, an occasion to achieve a dream left behind, or an instance to mend a wrongdoing.

The Lord, in all of His mercy and goodness, always grants to us the grace to try again. A second chance to conquer and win, with all the wisdom learned from past experiences. What would you do over again? How would you change your life? This is a time of new beginnings. Now is the second chance to heal broken relationships, to start fresh with love, determination, and prayer.

Find confidence within your heart and let it guide you to strive for your innermost and beautiful dreams and goals. "He did it with all his heart, and prospered."—2 Chronicles 31:21.

What you set your heart upon surely will be yours. Henry David Thoreau wrote, "I learned this, at least, by my experiment: that if one advances confidently in the direction of his or her dreams, and endeavors to live the life which they have imagined, they will meet with a success unexpected in common hours."

Persistence, to me, is a great word. Nothing in the world can ever, ever take the place of persistence. If you keep on going, keep on trying, again and again, chances are you will meet success.

The journey of a thousand miles begins with one single step. So, little by little and inch by inch, closer to your goal you will be . . . as long as you don't give up!

Have a strong faith and a heart that knows that with time and patience your goals will unfold before your eyes. I believe that God rewards the patient and persistent person. He has good reason for every delay He allows to come our way. God has great plans for you; in His perfect time He will reveal them.

Build on faith rather than doubt. See the endless possibilities that are ahead. There is no limit to what you can accomplish, no ambition too large, and no dream too far. It all starts with the right attitude. Nothing can stop a person from achieving his or her true desire if they begin with, and continue to keep, a positive frame of mind.

Pray for the Lord's will in all of your endeavors. In all ways acknowledge Him and He will direct you toward success. "In his heart a man plans his course, but the Lord determines his steps."—Proverbs 16:9.

Leave the past behind. You can't change history, so learn from the events of the past and then move on.

If you spend your precious time fretting about what might have been or what could happen, you can lose the joy and wonder that only this sweet day can bring. Do not worry—God's grace is new each morning.

We all have been given a second chance. This year holds for us, dear readers, a new and exciting chapter in our lives. Write down, today, a detailed list of your own special hopes, plans, and dreams for the future. Aim high, for the aim, if reached this year or next, makes life great.

With unflinching steadiness, march on your path believing that you have a loving Father who will be your guide, your helper. And He is the Giver of all that is good and beneficial for your life.

When you turn to Him and make Him your partner, He will pour new life into your being. All things will become fresh and new, and you will succeed.

Offer Words of Encouragement Wherever You Go

How can you begin to thank someone who has touched your life in a special way; someone whose encouragement, belief in your abilities, and confidence was a major turning point in your life? Matthew 25:40 says, "I tell you the truth, whatever you did for one of the least of these, my little ones, you did for me."

When you help, support, and uplift others, even in small ways, you serve God.

Encouragement, to me, is a beautiful word. Webster defines it as "to impart courage or confidence, to give support to." Isn't that what we all need—courage to continue on, confidence to do your best, and support to know that you are never alone?

Everyone needs encouragement. We must comfort one another, strengthen and build each other up. By giving encouragement, we sow the seeds of faith, hope, and love in another's heart. And as I read in the Scripture, "You can do all things through Christ who strengthens you." Leading others to a full and happy life by giving them the very best of the wisdom you have learned will give your own life so much more meaning and joy.

Look for the good in people and genuinely compliment them. Speak positively. Thank them for the kind gestures that they do, noticing when a child accomplishes a small task, when a neighbor lends a helping hand, or when a teenager brightens your day with their enthusiasm. Motivating words can help people affirm their own worth and cause them to believe in themselves.

Send someone a card to cheer them up, a photograph of your child, or a little book of motivating quotes. Pass on your positive spirit, a kind word, a helping hand, or a warm hug to a friend. Good deeds such as visits to a hospital or nursing home can encourage and bring hope to so many. Even a smile can make someone's day great. It takes only a fleeting moment, but its memory can last forever.

So many lives can be enriched and saved from despair through showing love and faith in them. Have a generous heart and encourage someone else to achieve his or her heart's desire. One person can make a difference. Mother Teresa said, "If you can't feed a hundred people, then feed just one." Vitality springs from sharing and being committed to another human being.

A life full of dreams can be realized one by one with encouragement from a mentor or friend. The voice of reassurance saying, "You can make it," "It will be all right," "God is with you," "I know you'll succeed," "With God, nothing shall be impossible," can set you on the right track, filling you with vim and vigor and renewed excitement to accomplish your goals.

You know what that kind of positive encouragement can do for a person. That's why I'd like to be that positive voice for you.

I have been given wonderful encouragement and advice, and because of that blessing I will forever be grateful. I think one of the things that has meant most to me is that someone believes in me and was willing to say so.

What a privilege, and a blessing, to pass on these wonderful words of encouragement to you. I read with love and amazement your lovely letters, dear readers. You are so special, so kind. Your love of God, the beauty of His creation, your willingness to share and care have encouraged my life and, I know, the lives of those with whom you come into contact.

I love you, and may you be blessed with all the good things God has to give.

God's Love Is Shared by All Who Love

I am always overwhelmed by the kindness of strangers. While I was taking a walk with my husband and daughters one afternoon, a kind woman ran out of her house and waved for us to stop. In her hand she was holding something. "I wonder what she has?" I thought. With a smile, she handed me two beautiful hair scrunchies that she had made and said, "I am a seamstress, and I told my husband that the next girl with long hair that I see walk by, I'm going to give these to her."

We were having dinner at a local restaurant and we started talking to the couple seated next to us about home decorating. After dinner that evening these "strangers" invited us to their home for coffee, and now five years later we are dear friends.

When our daughter was born, we received dozens of lovely cards, gifts, and good wishes from you, my dear readers. Many even remembered her first birthday!

Acts of love, gestures of kindness, deeds of thoughtfulness . . . blessed are they who care and share.

Greet each morning with a smile, face the day with a reverence for the many opportunities it holds, and approach your work with zeal. Be filled with faith, hope, and charity. And live without greed, anger, envy, or unpleasant thoughts.

Never neglect to be generous to the needy, have compassion for those who are less fortunate, be courteous to everyone, and have love in your heart for all of mankind. Give hope to the hopeless, friendship to the friendless, and encouragement to the ones who need encouragement. I know that "He who would be the greatest among you must become the servant of all." Genuine happiness comes when you do something kind for someone else.

Sometimes, if you have been hurt by family members or have felt neglected by friends or betrayed by coworkers, you may begin to feel that everyone will disappoint you—though I have learned that this is not true. If others have betrayed your trust, you clam up, walk around with your head down, and keep your distance from everyone so you won't expose yourself to that pain again. That is the time I apply the Word of God, which says, "Forget those things that are behind you. Press on."

There are wonderful, true people who will care and whom you can rely on. Don't let the handful of selfish people ruin your faith in humanity. Be secure in knowing who you are and be at peace and in fellowship with God's men. Continue to have hope. Persevere. Have faith, hold your head high, and smile. The world is really full of good and kind folks.

I read that the Bible says, "Perfect love casts out all fear." So keep your mind on the good promises of God's Word, and above all, live it. It won't do you any good to live any old way and expect good company. I know Jesus said, "If you love me, you will keep my commandments."

Love is not a special way of feeling, though lovely feelings come now and then. But real love is a commitment to live and care for another person. When that love is God's love, it reaches out to all the people around you automatically. You just can't help caring and sharing from the heart. That is why I care for you, dear readers. My heart longs to share the depths of a life surrendered to God's love. There is nothing like it on earth. I would rather be alone than to be where Jesus would not want me to be. I would rather be rich in His spirit than be rich by illicit gain. This is the love that casts out all fear. So, beloved, let us love one another, for love is of God and everyone that loves knows God.

Have Faith That You'll Succeed, and You Will

I have a dream . . . You have a dream . . . Perseverance will see that dream come true.

Each one of us, deep within our hearts, carries the seed of a secret dream. Together, let's uncover those hidden desires, for your dreams, hopes, and aspirations are the gardens of our future. Let your dream grow and blossom into a beautiful reality. Sail to uncharted lands, open your heart to the heavens, and soar far above any obstacle. Live your dream!

Our lives are formed by our goals and dreams. Take the first step in realizing your ambitions. The time is now. With a leap of faith, start by believing in yourself. "Self-trust is the first secret of all success," said Ralph Waldo Emerson.

Think well of your aspirations. You were born to achieve.

God knows your needs and true desires. He put those aspirations into your heart for a reason and He wants you to achieve them all. Good dreams are God-given. "God is able to make all grace abound toward you."—2 Corinthians 9:8.

Position yourself to receive His will and it will make all the difference in your life. God loves you. Walk in His light and He will never steer you wrong.

God wants your talent to shine and delights when you begin to express your inner thoughts. He put within you the strength, ability, and wisdom needed to succeed. At times, it's difficult for us to continue toward our dreams. But hold on. Adverse conditions can turn around for the good.

Rise above criticism. Do not allow anyone or anything to steal your dreams. The thief can come in the disguise of people, circumstances, or negative words. "Give up on that idea," "It'll never work,"

"That's unrealistic," some may say.

Zealously protect your dreams. Do not let a five-minute spiel of negativism or ridicule spoil your positive outlook on your bright future. Keep away from people who try to belittle your ambitions. Small people always try to do that, but the really great ones make you feel that you, too, can become great.

People who say it can't be done shouldn't interrupt those who are already beginning to do it. Acquaint yourself only with those who will support your dreams.

If you have a dream, dare to believe in it and try it. Faith in yourself will give you the confidence to make things happen. Believe that you can succeed and you will be amazed at the results. "We grow great by dreams," Woodrow Wilson said.

Always do your best. Rewards don't come without sacrifice. What you plant now, you will harvest later. Work hard. You can accomplish your grand vision through stubborn perseverance. Be like a postage stamp—stick to your goals until they are attained. Anything of value in life is worth exerting effort to reach. Never give up.

Consider long and hard the dreams you have chosen for your precious life. We all live in a world that is full of possibilities . . . a new career, a new place to live, and a new relationship with God. Your horizon is limitless. "The future belongs to those who believe in the beauty of their dreams," said Eleanor Roosevelt.

Close your eyes for a moment now, dear readers. Imagine yourself as you would like to be, doing all you want to do. Whatever your own sweet dreams may be, fix them in your mind, pursue them with all your heart, and watch yourself become just what you believe. Each day, take one step further toward that goal. One sunny morning you will awaken to find that you are the person you dreamed of becoming, doing all that you wanted to do, because you had the courage to believe in your potential and to hold on tight to the beauty of your dreams.

Your Heart Can Lift You to Greater Heights

There was an Olympic pole-vaulter who was a phenomenal jumper and did what most thought was impossible to do. Someone asked him how he was able to exceed every record ever set. And he answered, "First I throw my heart over the pole and my body naturally follows." Heart . . . that is the key.

Follow your heart. The epitome of excellence I found is in God and He assures me in Jeremiah 29:13, "You shall seek me and find me when you shall search for me with all your heart."

Don't compromise yourself. You are of great worth and have a great God-given capacity for achievement. We all have something in our lives we want to accomplish. It might be the beginning of a new career or it might be to create a closer family bond.

Every successfully reached goal must be pursued with all your heart. Believe in your God-given abilities and begin. You can succeed if you believe you can! Sam Walton, founder of Wal-Mart, said, "If people believe in themselves, it's amazing what they can accomplish." First, you must love what you desire to do, then love what it will do for others. Do all things with love. Love is an important ingredient to any success. Without it, life is empty; life is a struggle. But with it, your life has great meaning. Once you have learned to love, you will have learned to live and can live with greatness.

Fears are not obstacles. They are merely the stepping stones to success. We may worry about being in uncomfortable situations but, sometimes, they can become the impetus to greater achievement.

The mother eagle builds the foundation of her nest with sharp sticks and then lines it with grass and lambskin. The little baby eagles are born and love that soft nest. Mother eagle searches for food and brings it back to the comfortable nest. Oh, what a life those baby eagles have. But when it comes time for them to grow up, mother eagle grabs that lambskin and throws it out of the nest. Out come the grasses, and the eaglets then try to get comfortable on the sharp sticks.

Life has become a little miserable in that nest. And so the eaglets are compelled to climb up on the edge. Then they grab mother eagle's feathers, holding on as she soars off the rocky cliff. Then, believe it or not, she shakes them loose. The eaglets tumble head over heels toward the ground as she screams to them to fly. They flap their wings and are able to catch the current and soar on to adulthood, as the mighty eagles God meant them to be.

Achieving anything of value is a fight. Don't take "no" for an answer. Keep going and reach for the moon. Work hard and be determined and you can achieve anything you set your mind to do. The road to your goals can be packed with as much joy as the final destination will be. Do not rush through life. Patience can allow us to experience fully what is happening now, at this very moment, even as we have an eye on the future. Keep your goal in sight. When the reward is visible, patience comes more easily. There is a season, a place, and a time for everything. Relish your wonderful life now.

With prayer and patience we can reach the heights. Whenever I want to achieve, I first pray about it and then take a little more time to pray about it. If I feel God's leading, I do as in Proverbs 3:5, 6: "Trust in the Lord with all your heart and lean not to your own understanding. In all your ways acknowledge Him and He will direct your path" . . . with all His heart.

Geese Teach the Importance of Helping Others

The next time you happen to see geese flying along in a V formation, you may be interested to learn what science has discovered about why they fly in that unusual way.

As each bird flaps its wings, it creates an uplift for the bird immediately following. By flying in a V formation, the whole flock adds at least 71 percent greater flying range than if each bird flew on its own. The birds fly farther when they fly together than if they flew alone. Each goose gets help from the previous one, so they don't get as tired or use up as much of their energy.

Whenever a goose falls out of formation, it suddenly feels the drag and resistance of air in trying to go it alone and quickly gets back into formation to take advantage of the lifting power of the bird in front of him. When the lead goose gets tired, it rotates to the back of the formation and another goose takes the lead. The geese honk from behind to encourage those up in front to keep up their speed.

And if a fellow goose gets sick or is wounded, two geese fall out of formation and follow the injured bird down to help, feed, and protect it. They stay with it until it is able to fly on its own. Then they launch out to join another group.

We human beings should pay close attention to this valuable and beautiful lesson. Albert Einstein once said, "The most important question a human being could answer is 'Is the universe a friendly place?'"

We are here on earth to help one another. I read that the Bible says, "Let not everyone look after their own needs, but on the needs of another." There is strength built into your own character as you stay close in touch with the needs of others in your family or community. People who share a common direction and a sense of togetherness can get where they are going quicker and easier because they are traveling on the strength of one another.

Life is a journey. Going it alone is tough and hard. Unless we uphold each other and continually help one another, we will never have the fulfillment of a joy-filled life. Be kinder than you have to be, more compassionate and more loving.

When we give our best we increase the abundance of life in our children, our community, and in a larger sense, we create a rippling effect in the lives of strangers that we don't even see.

The soul grows when it is giving and receiving love. When people care and do good for others, that goodness gets returned over and over again.

A symphony is a beautiful thing to watch and much like life should be. As the conductor begins, each instrument is in harmony, one with the other. Then a violin begins to solo, and the other instruments create a beautiful accompaniment of background music. Then the violin fades into the background and the flute starts to solo as the other instruments accompany it.

The musicians do not vie for the lead and cause disharmony or walk off the stage because they are not in the lead for the moment. But they uphold each other to create beauty and form in the symphony. The musicians are much like the geese and much like our own family life, work life, and social life should be.

Sticking close to each other in genuine love, upholding each other in prayer, protecting each other in kindness, feeding each other with encouragement . . . always reading the music, the Word of God, and always watching Him . . . the Conductor.

Say Thank You to a Mentor by Becoming One

*T*here is a heavenly chain that starts with God and then, hand in hand, heart to heart, it comes down through the universe into time. Now, dear readers, my hand holds yours.

How many times have you heard these wonderful phrases: "She has influenced my life immensely." "He listened to me and gave me good advice." "I will never forget their kindness, belief in me, and understanding." "That unconditional love was just what I needed." "That little one showed me the simplicity of God." "Her inspirational words and caring heart helped me through difficult times." "He gave me a chance." "Her prayers were just what I needed."

Wonderful individuals have made a difference and positively influenced my life. Their encouragement, affection, and inspiration spurred me onward toward success and happiness. Many a time, I feel God sends a special person into our lives to be a great influence. He not only created us with a need for people, but He also supplies those wonderful people we need.

"Perfume and incense bring joy to the heart and the pleasantness of one's friends springs from his earnest counsel."—Proverbs 27:9.

Who is influencing your life? Who holds authority over you?

Influence changes a person. Wise advice and counsel can help you see problems in a more rational light. Loving thoughts, sweet words, and comfort can affect your entire life. A caring mentor's spoken words, their gentle embrace, and trusting belief in your ability to make the right decision can become like a road map by which you can navigate your life. Never let another rob you of your belief in yourself, of achieving your heart's desire or pursuing your dreams. Forget the negative statements of others. You are far above their hurtful tactics. People who feel inferior have to pretend everything they have is superior to anything that you have. Feel sorry for them. They have little else going for themselves. "True friends cherish each other's hopes. They are kind to each other's dreams," Thoreau wrote.

Many successful people today will say, "If it were not for the influence of a very special person, I wouldn't be where I am today." Everyone who accomplishes something extraordinary has had help from someone. Their love is the greatest influence.

The American Heritage Dictionary defines a mentor as "a wise and trusted counselor or teacher." Everyone should have a mentor, someone who brings something constructive to your life. It may be a parent, teacher, beloved friend, or relative. Young children can discover a persevering work ethic from their parents. Teenagers can master patient self-control from a grandparent. A new mother can observe tender caring from an experienced mother. And young men can learn how to overcome obstacles and secure achievement from successful business achievers or someone who has impressed the world with their way of life. Draw from others those lessons that may profit you. We learn from observing. Observe the characteristics that you admire in someone else, and be influenced to acquire them for yourself.

Share with another the wisdom you have gained through the years. By positively affecting even one other person, you can help to make this world a better place for us all. Do for others what was done for you. Pass it on. The joy you will receive by helping others achieve their dreams will bring great fulfillment into your life.

Read the encouragement of the greatest Friend and Mentor you will ever have. The anchor of God's Word holds your ship through every storm, and by holding His hand you can reach down and lift up another.

Have Hope; the Best Is Yet to Come

*A*s rain restores the earth after a dry and wilting time, hope restores the spirit.

I stood motionless in the department store looking at the 30" x 24" picture. The gold-framed lithograph was of two sweet angels nestled together. The picture made me smile. "How lovely," I said to myself.

At that time, I lived in a tiny two-room apartment, the same dreary space I had occupied for the past nine years. "Someday," I thought, "that beautiful angel picture will hang in my new home." With that vision tucked in my heart, I carried the angel picture to the register, paid for it, brought it back to my small apartment, and put it away in a closet.

I had dreamt for years how I would "one day" decorate my new home with cheerful designs and soothing color schemes. I even sketched where the furniture would go, and the fireplace. When I would go to the mall with my girlfriend Jeannette, I'd show her the floral bathroom ensemble that I liked and even a lovely dining room set that I admired. "Someday, I'll decorate my home with these things," I said. This went on for years!

When the voice of hope is in your heart, a transformation will begin. God is faithful to His promises. He will give you the desires of your heart. "The Lord will indeed give what is good . . . "—Psalm 85:12.

Hope can be defined as "waiting with certitude." Hope is a confident anticipation of something wonderful happening that has not yet come. Set high goals and do not be frustrated by difficulties or setbacks. The longest journey begins with only one step.

Maybe the odds of us succeeding are overwhelming. And the world may be filled with naysayers. But what gets us the victory is hope and sheer perseverance. Persistence pays off and opens the door to success. Hope pushes ahead when it would be easy to quit. Through hope we have joyful expectation that if we hold on, endure, and trust in God, we will get through even the darkest times.

History is packed with people who held on to hope, despite the odds. Alexander Graham Bell was laughed to scorn when he began his invention of the telephone. Beethoven composed most of his music during the years of his steadily worsening hearing loss, but his greatest composition, the Ninth Symphony, was written when he was completely deaf. He had in his heart the tone of each note. Helen Keller, blind and deaf, graduated with honors and went on to become a world-renowned author, lecturer, and coveted guest of many presidents of the United States. Keller said, "The world is full of suffering. It is also full of the overcoming of it." Hope regards problems, big or small, as opportunities.

I once heard a Shaker quote that has remained with me: "Hands to work and hearts to God." If we all directed our thoughts, hopes, and fears to Him, life would seem much simpler.

The next time disappointment threatens a dream of yours, I hope you will remember the story of the "angel picture." It was bought in hope, way before any possibility of a home was evident, and in faith and in trustful love.

Today, that sweet picture hangs in the foyer of my home. The green-and-burgundy floral bathroom ensemble I looked at so long ago now adorns my bathroom, and last week that lovely and inviting dining room set was delivered. Impossible, one may think. But oh, no . . . Nothing is impossible with God. With hope anchored in our hearts, He brings forth blessings far greater than we, with limited scope, can imagine. And so for you, dear readers, if you let Him, He will work miracles, as He did for me. Just keep the faith. He delights to show Himself faithful.

What You Say Tells People Who You Are

Before I begin each essay, I pray that the Lord will give me the right "words" to write that will touch the heart of each one of you and give you the secrets I've found for success in living.

Today, I am sharing one of my greatest secrets: Say only the things that you want to happen in your life. The words you express are the windows to your heart. "For out of the abundance of the heart the mouth speaks."—Matthew 12:34.

What you say says a lot about you. We reveal so much, just in everyday conversation. Words are our primary source of communication. They are powerful tools that should be used with extreme wisdom. Words that are encouraging and spoken in love can bring about a new awakening into the lives of others. When you speak with love, you plant strength, hope, and the power of transformation into another person's heart.

God wants us to communicate for the good of all. Phrases like "Good work," "Can I help?" "I'm proud of you," "It is going to be all right," and "I love you" can be music to the recipient's ears. Your words can comfort, help, and inspire, and can be like a healing oil poured over the body of another. Each time we speak positive thoughts, we deliver our own souls into the realm where all things are possible. Hopeful words are like a pebble that is dropped into a lake, creating circles upon circles of sound waves, ever expanding the joys of life.

You create the atmosphere around you. The words that come from your lips can bring happiness to yourself and those with whom you come into contact. Speak words of kindness, consideration, and encouragement. Soon, you will begin to act and think on that basis.

Grab for those words that are good, lovely, and productive. If a negative word comes into your mind, immediately cancel it out and replace it with a positive thought and phrase.

Consider the words that are used when talking to our precious children. Criticism and putdowns, even when delivered "in fun," can hurt feelings and stunt the growth of a healthy self-image. Words spoken in anger can deeply wound and have lasting effects. "Let no corrupt communication proceed out of your mouth, but that which is good to the use of edifying, that it may minister grace unto the hearers."—Ephesians 4:29. If your words do not build up or encourage another, it is better to say nothing at all.

Taking the time to wish others a good day or spending a moment praising a child or encouraging a friend not only displays to others that we care, but also shows them how to care, too. The cheer we spread will bring forth fruit in due season.

Love grows as it is given away. Unlike many things, love just multiplies and there is always more to give as well as to receive, so long as our hearts remain open.

So "say it" with love. Take time to really care; give honest answers from the heart. "A word aptly spoken is like apples of gold in settings of silver."—Proverbs 25:11.

Affirm only the best for yourself. You are worthy to receive all that you ask. You can have what you say and your body will obey your words. You can talk yourself into anything. So, be transformed by the renewing of your mind and by the words of your own mouth.

Right now, say, "I am happier than I have ever been in my life because . . . " Fill in the space. Say exactly what you want, and then go and do it! Start now to create beautiful friendships, ladders to success, and a joy-filled life.

Loved Ones Live Forever in Our Hearts

Though some of our loved ones are no longer with us here on earth, they can still live inside of our hearts and our minds.

Those we love are never really gone. We can experience them in so many ways—by their dynamic personality, through the friends they cared about and the dreams they shared. And the memory of their words can give us strength to face the challenges that lie ahead.

I can still hear my mother's voice ringing in my ear: "I just want you to be happy."

Life is short. Do not waste a passing moment on discouragement. Out of the time we are allotted, we must choose to be happy and to spin from it love, goodwill, and eternal friendships.

What will you do and how will you spend your precious time?

Begin your day today and every day by giving thanks. Set aside time to think about and to focus on your many blessings. Thankfulness is guaranteed to chase away the blues. Be grateful that you have your health, friends, freedom, food, children, a spouse, dreams, ambitions . . . the list goes on and on. If you resolve to appreciate all that you have going for you, you will be able to move forward toward the life that God intended for you. Gratitude is the greatest of virtues and the quickest access to the joy of life.

You have only one life to live. Do what makes you and those you love happy today—not next month or next year. Do not procrastinate. Do it now.

Today is your day. Contribute to it all that you can. Reach out to others. If you can make the most of what you can control in your life each day and make a positive difference to somebody else's life, then that's a great thing.

Have the courage to take action. Do not be afraid. Many a time, when my heart beat the loudest, when my hands shook the most, and I wanted to get up and run, that was the time that I stuck it out and in the end found success. You never know what you can do unless you try. Have high hopes, for what you think about and dream of becoming you will become.

Time passed cannot be regained. There is no time like the present to take action.

Live one day at a time; each second is a unique opportunity. No day repeats itself precisely like the last. In the case of a difficult day, that is good. But most of our days are good days. They are hours full of promise.

A single smile brought to someone else's heart is always doubled on its return trip to you. Smiles and sincere compliments are affordable gifts on anyone's budget. Give them freely and watch them return in the wrappings of peace and contentment. God gives to us His love each day. His magnificent love lives on and on, and yours can, too.

Whenever I feel down or apprehensive about going after a dream or a goal, my mother's words and the memory of her life forge me onward.

I recall how quickly life can be taken away. That knowledge alone is enough to enjoy the present and to live my life, each waking hour, to the fullest. I know that's the way my mother would have wanted it.

Then, once again, I hear her sweet voice in my ear, asking me if I'm OK and if I am happy. In a single breath, I feel the words building inside of me and they come to me in a whisper. I say them to her as prayer and as praise, "Yes, Mom, I am so happy. Thank you for my life."

In the evening, when I close my eyes to go to sleep, I say a prayer of thanks to God for granting me another precious day.

Stay Focused on Your Goal and Persevere

*W*alking along the beach on a glorious, sun-filled day, I spotted a large, unusual, and almost compelling rock on the sand at the edge of the water. Through the center of the deep-coral-hued stone was a large hole. So grand, in fact, was the opening, it looked like a great ring. "How strange," I thought to myself, musing on how it came to be.

Water . . . time and time again, water had lapped against the hard stone. Wave after wave of the ocean's crystal-blue water splashed through the opening of the rock like a man-made fountain.

With a flash of insight I understood, and a favorite quotation from Shakespeare came to my mind: "Much rain wears the marble." It was the soft, clear water that had worn the giant hole through the tough stone. The gentle waves of the ocean, with a steady flow of persistence, can wear away even the mightiest rock.

How easily we sometimes give up on a dream that seems so very difficult to achieve or impossible to attain. Through the lessons of the ocean, God reaffirms to us one of life's most important truths: With persistence, it is possible to triumph and make a way through all impossibilities.

Be persistent and steadfast in pursuing your goal, even if you come up against a brick wall. You, too, can wear away all obstacles. Dreams come true when you stick to your ambitions. Keeping at it gets results. Many of the great minds of the world know the amazing power of persistence. "Meditate on my word day and night and let it not depart from out of thy mouth and then you shall have good success."—Joshua 1:8.

The root meaning of the word "succeed" means "to persevere and to follow through." The power to hold on and endure in spite of any obstacle, while trying and trying again, is the quality of a winner. If you have ordinary talent but have extraordinary perseverance, all things are attainable. Perseverance is the one word for anyone who expects success.

Refuse to get discouraged. Franklin D. Roosevelt persevered, and his determined spirit made him the president of the United States, even without the use of his legs. The challenges that you face should only spur you to greater efforts. When everything seems to be going wrong, that is the most crucial time to practice the "never quit" principle. Ninety percent of all failures result from individuals who quit too soon. Most people can really excel when things are going well, but there is a special group of people who can excel when things are not so easy. It is not how many times you fall that counts, it's how many times you get up.

Who can tell how close you are to your goals? When your dreams seem so far away, keep on going, stick with them, and take another step . . . they actually may be closer than you think. Do not give up; all achievements require time and tenacity. It is not to the swiftest, nor to the strongest, but to he who endures.

There are no obstacles as absolute as solid rock. There is nothing as gentle or more powerful than the pure water of love as it is poured over the person or problem in your life. Poured in faith every day, it will slowly create the miracle of persistence.

If you have found you have a rock of resistance somewhere in your life, I want you to do something for me to be an ever-present token of your victory. The next time you are walking by the seashore, look down at the many little stones on the beach. Once they were giant obstacles that the wondrous, clear water wore away.

Pick up a pebble, hold it in your hand, and feel how smooth and lovely it has become. The Bible says, as children of God, we are as God. With perseverance and love we can overcome and change any irritation or barrier, until it becomes as that smooth, round stone in your hand.

God Gently Guides Us If Only We Will Listen

"If I knew then what I know now . . . ," my mother would often say. As a young girl, I didn't understand what she meant, but now I do.

If we had foresight into the future, we might have done things differently in the past. Choices that now seem so clear would have been much more easily made then, and decisions of utmost importance would have been rightly chosen.

But God has in all fairness given us the freedom to make our own choices. I know we have a Heavenly Father who said, "I will be with you, even in you." He never makes mistakes. When we are young, God gives us a conscience that speaks within us in a still, small voice. A quiet nudging that says, "Uh, uh, don't do that," or "Wait a second, this isn't right." Listen to that inner voice. I like to remember that the Bible says, "Be still and know that I am God."

You are a wonderful creation. You deserve the best. Love your life, which God so generously gave. And in everything you do, pick up His great book of instruction, the Bible. Look on it each day with positive and unlimited possibilities to do what is good and profitable for you. Believe in your own potential to become wise and prosperous.

Consider this great book of examples and your own unique situation in life. Use those examples to guide you to make the right decisions now.

I've heard it said, "Do not follow where the broad path may lead, instead forge ahead on that narrow path that others may see the wisdom of your right choices." Hold on to your dreams. You are filled with many special qualities that have yet to be discovered. You can achieve all that you imagine if you are willing to be taught. Take problems one by one to the Word of God. Never make decisions in a panic of distraught nerves, tension, or fear.

The early Quakers had a unique approach to getting answers that we, today, would be wise to follow. They would sit in perfect silence before the Lord, letting every outward sense become still. Then they'd drop their problem into the great, deep pool of God's knowledge and serenely wait. Not very long after, it was said, the answer became "crystal clear."

Adversity can be a wonderful opportunity to gain insight. Trials may come to awaken you to possibilities and make you realize that there are better paths to take. Be unafraid to see what others cannot. Determination and perseverance can make the mountain move.

Your qualities are many. Fulfill your destined role of faith, where the realm of the impossible is possible. Life is a precious gift; bask in it and make every second count.

Ask God to give you the wisdom you need to make the right decisions and then read the Bible carefully, pausing at each verse and letting your mind bring the people and situations alive to you. Compare them with the situations you find yourself in today, and consider the outcome.

I read that Solomon said in Ecclesiastes, "There is nothing new under the sun." Gain the great wisdom found in Proverbs and apply it to today. You will find your understanding being positively enlightened and will find yourself making fewer errors.

Begin now to point others to this treasure. Teenagers need to read Psalm 119. Help the little children in your life become aware that they, through His wisdom, may make the right choices and fewer mistakes. Help them to memorize the words that can calm and redirect.

Looking to an all-knowing and wise Heavenly Father whose guidance never fails, you will also find yourself saying, "If I knew then what I know now," with everlasting joy, because you will have within your heart overcoming and victorious wisdom.

God's wisdom . . . Oh, what a treasure.

See Yourself Wherever You Want to Be

*I*f it's to be, it's up to me! How high I aim or how far I seek or what mountain tops I reach depends on me . . .

The first step to getting the things that you want is to decide what you want. Then pray and talk to God about it. What He wants to hear is your motive for achieving it. If your motive is good and pure, not selfish and self-glorifying, if it will glorify Him by being according to His will and make others happy, then you can have it.

With enthusiasm and drive you can do anything!

Go toward your dreams with abandon, give it all you've got, and life will give all it has to you. One of the few things in life over which we should have total control is our attitude. Don't let the wrong attitudes of others put an obstacle in your way. You will always have people raining on your parade. Just pop up a big, bright-as-the-sun, yellow umbrella of joyful purpose and keep on marching and singing in the rain!

Never react to other people's wrong attitudes. Always save your reaction until you talk to God about it. Then, after looking into His loving, understanding, and smiling face, I'm positive you will be an overcomer. I love the saying: "There is nothing that's going to happen today that God and I can't handle together."

Each morning, we have two choices: to embrace a positive outlook or a negative one. Remember, "If it's to be, it's up to me." If something disturbing happens, you can be the victim or the victor. Learn from it. If someone is complaining, try to point out the positive side of the situation. If you but look, you'll find that there are always streams in the desert. You have the choice of how you will react to situations, how others will affect your mood, and whether you let the situation control you or you control it.

Perhaps you have been put down so much in your life that you believe it's no use trying. But encourage yourself and your loved ones to move forward. Continue to grow and learn. Wisdom is never out of style. It is ever of the greatest of value, and therefore so are you who have acquired it.

Decide that you will succeed and affirm that fact continually by saying so. The Bible says, "You can have what ever you say if you believe in your heart and doubt not."

Your imagination creates your reality. We drive, fly, and climb mountains by faith. Visualize your accomplishments, apply the same simple faith, and you can achieve great success. If we all did the things we are capable of doing, we would astound ourselves. Never give up, you are closer to your goal than you think.

Thomas Edison tried more than ten thousand times before he invented the light bulb. When Edison was interviewed about the fact that he failed thousands of times in his attempt, he eliminated the word "failed" and replied, "I've had thousands of learning experiments that didn't work. I had to run through enough learning experiences to find a way that did work." In other words, he said to himself, "If it's to be, it's up to me."

You can be the person you are longing to be and achieve the dreams you hold in your heart. Just check your motive and attitude and make sure they are in harmony with God's spirit, and say again in your new heart, "If it's to be, it's up to me." With joy you can take hold of your life. Remember that all things are possible to those who believe.

Begin anew and restore those faded dreams, broken friendships, those youthful plans to impress the world, with love. Live joyously and unselfishly and in time you will be wonderfully surprised.

Be That Special Person in Someone Else's Life

I once heard a story about a little boy who was afraid of storms. On a dark and rainy night, with thunder raging and lightning flashing, his mother heard him calling out to her from his bedroom for the third time.

The mother went into the room and the boy cried, "Mommy, I am scared of the storm . . . I need you." The mother confidently replied, "Don't worry, honey, you'll be just fine. I told you before . . . God is with you." And the boy said, "But I need you . . . I need God with skin on him."

Oh, what a revelation came to that parent. To your children and to others, as a believer, remember that you, too, are "God with skin on him."

Many a time, I feel that the Lord brings a special person into our lives to be a wonderful influence, a mentor, a kind heart who understands and knows the Word of God. We can work miracles in the lives of others with a squeeze of the hand, a shared prayer, and genuine love.

The love of true friendship is a universal force. But friendships need tending to. Spending time together can do remarkable things. How lovely it is to sit and have a cup of tea or coffee and chat with a dear friend. Problems always seem lighter when they are shared with someone who cares.

Carve out an hour or two in the rush of life to spend with your friends. Invent creative ways to stay in touch. Remember birthdays, anniversaries, and other milestones. Have lunch one day every other week with a different friend. Invite a neighbor over for hot chocolate one evening. Do errands together. Grocery shopping is fun in pairs. Just calling to say "Hi" is important.

Be a good listener. This is the only way to really get to know someone. Ralph Waldo Emerson said, "A friend is a person with whom I may be sincere. Before him I may think aloud." Give moral support. Volunteer to accompany a friend if she needs to go to the doctor or dentist. Offer to baby-sit for a busy mom and give her a break. Life becomes fuller and richer when you help others, and that keeps you from thinking about your own problems.

Recently, I had an issue I was struggling with. When I explained the situation to my friend Anna Marie, she laughed aloud. Then I smiled and thought, "It really is silly," and that put the issue into perspective. I dismissed my worry.

There are storms in everyone's life. The waves are high and seem to engulf us. That's when we need God with skin on him to give us a hug and look into our eyes and say, "You are an overcomer. Watch patiently while God takes care of this for you." Let us be to others what we want so much for ourselves.

We all need someone older and wiser who loves us to share our deepest thoughts with, someone who will always guide us aright.

Let us spend much time with the Friend who sticks closer than a brother does. Read His love letter to us, the Bible. Soak up the honey of His Word and become soothing, sweet, and wise. Then, we can go out into the world, walking and talking and loving as God . . . with skin on him.

Children See Life's Delights As God Would

*T*he sun comes out when they smile . . . their laugh lights up the room with delight, and their sweet embrace melts our hearts. Our precious little girls, blessings from God above.

This year has gone by ever so quickly, from bassinet to walking, from bottles to grilled cheese sandwiches.

Our daughters' eyes are so full of wonder and innocence. I watch them grow day by day, becoming their own persons, full of discovery, joy, and love. They teach me to take a second look at what sometimes becomes so commonplace.

Little ones can give their parents insight into the important things in life and make their journey happy, wonderful, and fulfilling again. Children have a positive attitude, it seems, at all times—except when they stumble and a few tears fall, but they quickly forget and go on again full of smiles, laughter, and joy each day.

They are always fair and treat others equally. They are compassionate, always giving with abundance. Kids don't hold grudges; they forgive and forget.

To them nothing is impossible; they are not afraid to reach for the moon. Their eyes sparkle with their own special aspirations. They know that they will make a difference in this world, and the sky is the limit. Imagination is the key to the door of their future. Their thoughts are busy building dreams.

A child busily pursues many interests and works hard at getting our full attention. Vigorously they follow in our footsteps everywhere we go. Their attributes of persistence and delight help them to achieve all that they desire.

How children enjoy the beauty of God's nature, every little petal, each blade of grass, and all the beautiful flowers. A tiny ant is a wondrous and fascinating thing. Catching fireflies in a jar, seeing ladybugs in a row, and hearing the chipmunk's chatter all make children clap their hands with amazement. Crunchy autumn leaves and the sound of soft rain against the window is a child's symphony.

Children enjoy each and every precious moment. They don't worry about tomorrow; they just happily play and enjoy today. A simple bedtime story and warm cookies and milk will make a child so content. How true that is for grownups also.

Children are attracted to good people and love close friendships. They are definitely little individuals, independent, not just following the crowd. How they appreciate the importance of family—with one hand in Mommy's, kids are not satisfied until the other hand is in Daddy's.

Let us adhere to children's values, determining to never let this family circle be broken. What a sense of accomplishment and pride they take in the simple achievement of joining Mommy, Daddy, and baby together. As we look at each other it becomes an unspoken vow of joy, love, and thanksgiving.

I'd like to give you, dear daughters, the grace to keep your childlike delight all the rest of your life in all that you are striving for. I hope that your caring, gentleness, and sweetness will forever remain and that your happiness will affect generation after generation.

You both have brought so much joy into our lives; because of you, the sun is always shining. May the good Lord grant that we can become more like you in the innocence that envelops you, as from one coming so fresh from God's presence.

I will delight and refresh myself in the simple things of life, for I once heard that God is hidden in simplicity. He is not hidden very well in you, for I see Him every time you smile. Thank you, dear ones; we love you very much.

A Pollyanna? You Bet, and Glad to Be One

Because you have decided to speak positively, encourage others, and think about only those things that are good, have you been called a Pollyanna?

Years ago, actress Hayley Mills starred in a movie called *Pollyanna*. The story was about a young girl who moved to the United States from England to live with her aunt.

This young girl always looked at the positive side of each situation. She tried to make something good out of every adversity or disappointment. Because of her good nature, others began to scoff at her.

The reason Pollyanna came to the United States to live with her aunt was because her mother and father both died as missionaries in Africa and she was left homeless.

After disaster struck the town in which she lived, the townspeople realized how Pollyanna's optimistic attitude was helpful in changing the lives of the people in the entire village. Pollyanna made each person happier and helped them all see just how important living and giving are.

I remember a young girl who woke up one sunny day in May. The morning sun beamed through the windows while the birds chirped joyfully. It was the beginning of a great new day.

Suddenly a cloud came over the house. The young girl's first thought was to go to see her mother, who was asleep in the next room. As she walked down the narrow hallway to her mother's bedroom, an uneasy feeling crept over her. An inner voice deep down within her said, "Your mother is dead."

Frightened, she ran to her mother's room. The girl called out, "Mom! Mom!" No response. Frozen in fear, she cried and pleaded,

"Wake up, please wake up." Nothing moved. Not a sound. It was true; it really had happened.

In the blink of an eye, life was taken. Mother was dead. One week after the funeral, this young girl had to leave her home.

That could have been the beginning of a pessimistic, bitter, and discouraged outlook on life. Instead, I have chosen to use my painful experience to comfort, support, and encourage others. Yes, I am a Pollyanna. It is my choice to look upward. With the good Lord guiding me, I am in control of my own destiny.

From every experience a person has, one can grow spiritually. If you have gone through a catastrophe somewhere along the way, you can put out your hand and help another who may have had the same difficulties.

Choose to be optimistic and spread the joy of life to others. A wonderfully positive outlook will not only change you, but will lift up those around you.

As you become "A New You," a happier, more vibrant and positive individual, you may run up against scoffers who call you a Pollyanna. Then you can recall my story.

Through the years, because of the obstacles that I have had to overcome, I have become a better, wiser, and stronger person. So can you. Now, dear readers, I can say without hesitation that I have never been happier. I am truly blessed to be able to share with you my life's experiences, and there is much more to come.

Today, the sun once again shines in my eyes. In the heavens, my mother is smiling down, knowing that her youngest daughter is happy and being granted the desires of her heart.

We're Only Hurting Ourselves and the Ones We Love

Consider this chain reaction . . . The boss reprimands the husband; the husband comes home and argues with the wife. The wife scolds the boy, the boy yells at the dog, the dog barks at the cat, and the cat pounces on the mouse.

This is a funny scenario, but if we think about it, it's so true.

I read that doctors agree that a great percentage of diseases are caused by stress, nervousness, and un-forgiveness. Flying off the handle or holding a grudge can cause you great harm.

Why does a person hold anger within their heart, and what events precede the choice not to forgive and forget? A mother of five wrote to me via e-mail, "I have been so wounded and tired, that I could not see the sunshine, but it came out again because I found out that forgiveness is the key." That impressed me, as did another e-mail from a reader: "It has been my prayer for many years that people would learn to forgive others."

There is one trait that causes some people to stand out in a crowd. It is the attitude that they project to the world. We are what we choose to be. When we are at peace within, we love those who love and are caring to all. Truly love and respect your beliefs, so that you can give to others freely. Your beliefs motivate your actions. So what do you really believe in?

Be resilient when troubles and contradictions come. The word "resilience" is defined as the ability to recover quickly; buoyancy; to resume to an original shape after being stretched. How many of us, on the job or at family functions, have felt stretched to the snapping point? There is something to be said about the resilient person who refuses to hold the stress, instead calling on love and humor to resume being the calm and congenial person they choose to be. No matter what happens, try to laugh over it with loving understanding. Laughter can reduce problems and keep things in perspective.

Exercise helps to relieve stress. Make dinner thirty minutes or an hour later, and work out when you get home at the end of your business day. Walking on a treadmill, pedaling a stationary bike, or working out to a fitness video can do wonders for your mind and prepare you for the relaxing dinner ahead and family time after.

Pay no mind to negative comments or the hurtful tactics of others. Ignore them as you would a bad apple in a barrel. Don't look at them twice; keep on moving and never look back. When Abraham Lincoln delivered the Gettysburg Address in 1863, the opposition criticized him. Today it is praised, widely quoted, and recognized as one of the classic masterpieces of prose poetry.

Have faith in God. The hand that's guiding you knows what it is doing . . . the heart that beats for you has your best interest at heart. Place everything into God's hands at the beginning of the day and at the end of the day, and you will know that God has something better for you.

He can change the whole scenario: "The boss congratulates the husband, the husband brings flowers to the wife, the wife hugs the boy and says 'I love you.' The boy pats and plays with the dog, the dog snuggles down on the rug to sleep with the cat, and the cat has long ago let the mice run out of the house."

And peace and contentment settle down over the joy-filled home.

Success Grows from Your Beliefs

Vince Lombardi, the famous football coach, had a secret of success: God first, then family, then football. When he began coaching the Green Bay Packers, a defeated, dispirited football team, he told his players intensely, "We are going to have a great football team, we will win games and outplay any team that comes up against us."

How was this going to be done? Vince Lombardi pointed to his temple. The secret: What goes on in the mind is what will determine the outcome in your actions. Depending on how you think, your life can be anything you want it to be. Your thoughts eventually become manifested in your work.

That year, the Green Bay Packers won seven out of twelve games, their first winning season in twelve years. The next season they won the division title. And the third year they won the league championship. During a nine-year span, Lombardi guided the Packers to five NFL championships and motivated the athletes to perform to the height of their abilities.

With hard work, enthusiasm, and the Word of God being the power in your mind, you, too, can have all that you desire and can transform your dreams into actualities.

Positive thoughts create and inspire. They can physically strengthen you and energize your spirit. Bring joy to your heart by thinking on the promises of God. "Good thoughts bear good fruit," said James Allen. So accentuate the positive. Everyone is born with a teaspoonful of faith. It is up to you to develop this God-given gift into a great and powerful force in your life. Optimism infuses the mind with power. Seek out the positive and pursue it with gusto.

Your attitude toward whatever situation is presented to you will determine your outcome: "If it's to be, it's up to me." Thoughts determine victory or defeat. "Great men are they who see that the spiritual is stronger than any material force: that thoughts rule the world."— Ralph Waldo Emerson.

You know there is still set before us the tree of the knowledge of good and evil and the tree of life (the Word of God). Two trees. The knowledge of good and evil must be mixed, for it is all of man's works. The tree of life, which is God's will and God, is love. Let me feed on the tree of life, which is the Word of God, feed on His miracles, His joy, and His songs. For the fruit of whatever I feed on will be manifested in my life. The fruit of the tree of life is sweet, sweet, sweet.

One of my favorite sayings is, "If I do nothing there is nothing for God to bless." So, as Longfellow wrote, "Let us be up and doing with a heart," to make us great. (The last four words are mine.)

I cannot have strength for anything or be happy at all if I don't do this mandatory exercise that I read in Philippians 4:8: "Whatsoever things are just, whatsoever things are pure, whatsoever things are lovely, whatsoever things are of good report, if there be any virtue [strength], if there be any praise [happiness in your life], you must think on these things."

Meditate on this day and night and get strength by voicing out loud the things that you personally know fit these requirements. And let them bring to pass your success. Above all, I like to remember Philippians 4:13 and say it aloud: "I can do all things through Christ who strengthens me."

Chin Up; God Has Big Plans for You

Every good and beautiful purpose will come up against rejection and disappointment, uphill battles and opposition. But I always say, "When one door shuts, God opens a window." So forget what is behind and press on.

Eight years ago, with purpose in my heart, I phoned the New Haven *Register*, got an appointment, made my presentation at the right time to the right person, and God has blessed this effort ever since. Today my column, "A New You," is published in papers all over the country and read by millions of people each week.

The moral of my story: Don't ever, ever give up. God always has something better and more miraculous ahead. He never leaves His children desolate.

God weaves the fabric of our lives, creating a colorful calico of darks and lights—lives intertwined with ups and downs and hearts full of expectation. Don't get discouraged; with courage and hard work it will be a better tomorrow. Success is not so much knowing how to get to the top, but how to bounce back from the bottom. No matter what life brings you, you can come back with new vision. Even in our most difficult and painful times, God always keeps His promise that He will never give us more than we can bear. He gives comfort, peace, and joy.

Life sometimes gives us challenges. Make decisions with an open heart and determination. You can't just wish for success; a wish changes nothing. But a decision to pray and put your all to the task will change everything. You'll see things come out right in time.

People will forget what you say, forget what you did, but people will never forget how you made them feel. So treat everyone with respect, kindness, and sincerity. Life goes on and we realize, at certain points in our travels, that we get back in the same measure what we put forth. What you give out does come back around to you.

Check your motivation, attitude, and objective for what you are trying to accomplish as you reevaluate what you are trying to do. If you have thoroughly checked out these three things prayerfully and found each to be in the will of God, you cannot fail.

I know a child who was an orphan, and time and time again he was told he'd never amount to anything. Well, that young man didn't give up. He worked hard, earned a scholarship, and studied long hours. Eventually he graduated from Harvard and Yale. Today, that man is an achiever and a beacon to the community.

An old English proverb says, "Many things are lost for the want of asking." So, as I know Jesus said, "Ask abundantly that your joy may be full," and you will be pleasantly surprised.

Opportunities are never lost. Someone else will take the ones that you miss, so never quit when you are tired. Take one more step. The victors always say that it was worth it all when they have won. Dream grand dreams and then go out and create their reality. "The greatest achievements were at first and for a time dreams," wrote James Allen.

The great oak is hidden in the tiny acorn. And greatness resides in you. If you find God's purpose in your life and go after it with all your heart, soul, mind, and strength, you will become the person God created you to be: a servant to mankind and great in the eyes of the Lord.

We Are All Blessed with the Power to Choose

There are many things that occur in life that are beyond our under-standing. God set His laws when creation began. Gravity is one of them, and freedom of choice is another.

We are all responsible for our own existence. Each hour brings a new choice of action, an opportunity for growth, every choice a chance to build up or to tear down.

We must live one day at a time and be constantly prayerful to solve our problems one by one. Problems can be like a piece of sand in our shoe, irritating enough to do something about it. When a grain of sand gets into an oyster's shell, what happens? It begins to secrete a soothing liquid, covering that piece of sand and turning that irritation into a glowing pearl.

If something gets under your skin, you can let it become an ulcer or, by the application of wisdom and considerate words and actions, turn that irritation into a glowing gem. The choice is yours. Do not let anything spoil your outlook on life or your wonderful ability to overcome.

If you didn't receive the proper love, respect, or guidance as a child, you must be fearless enough to love yourself by receiving God's love, so freely given. Give yourself the respect you did not receive by choosing to be guided by God's Word. This can heal any wounds of the past and enable you to move forward to a better life.

Life is a summary of all of your experiences. When some of them are overwhelming and discouraging, it is time to simplify our scope. We must focus on doing the job at hand, the very best we can. Whatever we do in word or deed, do it as unto the Lord. Our journey here is to love

God and to love others as we love ourselves. God is the only one who can make sense of life. He said the life He gives us is eternal.

We are never alone as long as we have God. To turn our lives over to knowing and serving Him is the greatest thing we will ever do. We can never come to the end of the revelation of God's love and character. We'll never be able to say, "We will know the limits of His love," because there aren't any.

None of us were transformed from a baby to an adult overnight. So we must take God's Word bit by bit, applying it to the daily walk of our lives, like the oyster's soothing coating.

We must first know that we are here for a purpose: to know Him and to serve Him. When that purpose has been fulfilled, God takes us into another dimension, where the joys that the Lord has prepared for us await.

Those of us still here must choose daily the right choices that will deliver us to that reward. The right attitude will bring about the right choices. A reader from Louisiana has the right attitude. Even though he is on the list for a kidney transplant, he says, "Who am I to complain about the path God has chosen for me to walk?" That humble respect to God, no matter what the situation, is the beginning of greatness.

By starting our day with prayer, reading the Word and ending it with the same, holding our faith in God, whatever comes our way is the choice that leads to that eternal day.

I see how the lowly caterpillars shut themselves away in their cocoon. In secret, they are being transformed into a creature of beauty. In the same way, we pray and read God's Word each night, and then in the quietness of sleep, the glorious transforming power of His love changes us into the likeness of the Pearl of great price. Let us sell out to all else . . . to gain Him.

Happy Are Those of Us Who Serve Other People

A recent newspaper survey asked, "Who are the happiest people?" The top answers were:

1. A craftsman whistling over a job well done.
2. A child building castles in the sand.
3. A mother rocking her tiny baby.
4. A doctor who just finished a difficult operation and saved a life.

Spiritual, physical, and emotional well-being are the cornerstones of a truly joyous person's life.

A joy-filled life begins with a deep appreciation of the opportunity to create beauty and achievement. The more thankful you are, the happier you will be. A grateful heart is a contented heart. Praise God for all the blessings He provides. Be aware each day of the priceless gifts He bestows upon us to make our life a pleasure.

Today comes but once, so utilize your hours wisely. Live simply; be content with what you have. A happy person is not a person in a certain set of circumstances, but rather someone with a certain set of attitudes.

Develop an attitude of gratitude and be continually looking up to God. Happiness is being aware of His great love for you. Cheerfulness is a natural attribute of that awareness.

Let peace be in your heart. Where there is hatred, scatter love; where there is doubt, sow faith; and where there is darkness, bring light. Envy, judging others, and negative thoughts inhibit happiness.

Look for the best and cultivate a good sense of humor. People who look on the bright side of a situation are healthier. To laugh is to be young and to be like a child again. Laughter can lighten the load.

A noble purpose, a fulfilling career, and doing for others can take your mind off of yourself and give you the revelation of what's most important. And you will find that joy is the byproduct of your meaningful life.

Albert Schweitzer once said, "I don't know what your destiny will be, but one thing I know: The only ones among you who will truly be happy are those who will have sought and found how to serve." Happiness is found in giving.

Having a sincere concern for others is being in the image of God. "It isn't what you have or who you are or where you are or what you are doing that makes you happy or unhappy . . . It is what you think about," wrote Dale Carnegie. So one key to happiness, it seems, is to think positive thoughts.

God's presence in your life will bring you the greatest contentment. "When cares increase within me, your comfort gives me joy."—Psalm 94:19.

Bring your problems to the Lord. He gives hope, courage, and peace. A friend told me that William Branham said, "Your duty to God is to do right and your duty to yourself is to think right." The greatest honor you can give Him is to live gladly and joyfully because of the knowledge of His love and promises.

Every time you wake up, ask yourself, "What good things am I going to do today?" Remember: When the sun goes down, it will turn another page in the book of life during the night. When you wake up in the morning, the sun's rays will shine on a plain white sheet of paper in your book of life. Write upon it every new hour with a joy-filled pen all the praises that you can think of to thank your Heavenly Father.

Be happy, dear readers, and go out into the world to spread each day over with the golden glow of the joy of sharing and caring in the image of God.

Trust in God's Perfect Timing to Be Revealed

Nothing can stop the program of God. Each and every coincidence is God's perfect timing revealed. He has a plan, a purpose for the incidences and the direction of our lives that He allows it to take. God loves us for who we are, each one of us unique, with different talents and ambitions. Pursue your own special dreams. God never fails to give us inspiration.

"Delight thyself in the Lord and He will give you the desires of your heart."—Psalm 37:4.

Be persistent. If you knock on a door and nothing happens, sometimes you have to knock again and again and again. Mountains are created to be conquered. The courageous person is not discouraged by a problem; he is challenged by it.

Determination will see you through. Hang in there. The person who stays in the race is the only one who can eventually win the prize. Stick to your goal, even through a temporary setback. Every time you get four steps closer to success, even if you fall back a bit, with God's help, you'll end up one step ahead.

Learn from each experience and if you make a mistake, move on! Don't live in past failures. Time and energy applied to dwelling on the past takes away from the present victory. If you look behind you as you walk forward, what happens? You'll bump into something. Redirect your precious hours by making progress to achieve your grandest dream. Even if you just did one small thing a day, such as reading His Word, with that goal in mind, soon your dream will be a reality.

Don't ever let anyone tell you, "It can't be done." Let me be the first to say that without a shadow of a doubt, you can and will succeed. Keep that in your heart and mind at all times. Stay far, far away from negative forces and mockers. Shut them out! These detractors can kill any progress.

Form a winning team of people who support each other and encourage each other's dreams. Surround yourself with positive individuals who believe with you, and turn to them for strength when you need it.

Know what it is that you want. Have a definite goal and time frame by which you will achieve it. Then get things done! Do not procrastinate. This is your day, so make the most of it.

A friend of mine had the ambition to go back to school to get her doctoral degree. "But I'm not sure if I should," she said. "It will take so much time, and I'm not getting any younger." I replied, "How old will you be if you don't follow your dream and go back to school?" Begin to weave . . . God will give you the thread.

Keep on searching no matter how many times you are disappointed. Sometimes we wonder why things go wrong, but I have found, in many instances, the things that seem to go wrong begin to become blessings in disguise.

Looking on the bright side of a situation can bring a ray of sunshine to even the darkest day. One of my favorite Bible verses is, "It is always darkest before the dawn." Remember this passage when you are tempted to give up. Go after your heart's desires. It's never too late.

Believe in God, put yourself into His hands, and be amazed at your accomplishments. When your understanding is open to delight yourself in Him and your soul is in agreement, nothing is impossible.

Faith Lifts Us Over Obstacles

A little girl was born with a muscle missing in her foot and had to wear a leg brace. Through the years, her parents encouraged her to believe that her handicap was just a small obstacle to overcome.

They taught her that her attitude, belief in herself, determination, and persistence would ultimately bring victory. And most important, faith in God would bring contentment.

One day, the girl came home from school and said to her mother, "We had field day this afternoon and all the kids at school competed in races, jumping matches, and other events." Before the mother could encourage her daughter, the youngster exclaimed, " . . . and I won two of the races."

The mother smiled with pride and asked, "Which two races did you win? And how did you win over the others?" The girl replied, "Well, Mom, I had an advantage." The mother questioned, "Oh, what was that?"

Proudly the girl said, "My advantage was I had to try harder."

Dare to look hard at your goals. Given the circumstances we have been handed in life, we have to decide what is our most important goal. If it is for self-gratification, you will have to struggle alone. But if it is born from a love for others, done for God's glory, you will have all of heaven behind you.

The more you believe, the more you can achieve, because if you believe in something enough, you can make it happen. Belief is a positive—it draws out the best in you.

"If you can believe, all things are possible to Him that believes."—Mark 9:23. There is a power that comes when you expect the best. Your faith will make the desired results transpire according to God's perfect will.

Henry David Thoreau wrote, "I have learned this at least by my experiments: That if one advances confidently in the direction of his dreams and endeavors to live the life which he has imagined, he will meet with a success unexpected in common hours."

Impossible dreams? Nothing is impossible. Beethoven was completely deaf by age forty-six; nevertheless, he wrote his greatest music during the later years in his career. Franklin D. Roosevelt was paralyzed, but went on to become president of the United States and was elected four times. Shoe salesman Dwight Moody was a persistent, determined person, and Moody became one of the greatest evangelists of his time.

All our abilities are not always to be used for our own gain, but truly are gifts given to us for the betterment of our world. Talent is perceptible by anyone; the key to success is persistence—seeing something you want and going after it. "Nothing can take the place of perseverance. Talent will not; nothing is more common than unsuccessful men with talent. Genius will not; unrewarded genius is almost a proverb. Persistence and determination alone are omnipotent."—Calvin Coolidge.

Persistence and determination really describe "faith," faith in your goal and faith in God. I read of a young woman paralyzed from the neck down. But she had an outreach of encouragement to more than five hundred people. She dialed a telephone with a pencil in her mouth and listened to the trials of others as she cried and laughed on the other end of the receiver. This extraordinary woman offered encouragement, read poetry, and sang songs to them.

She said her life was full of joy and purpose because there was nothing better than giving compassion and lifting up another. A bright and shining star was given to so many.

There is something that every one of us can do, if we believe . . . and pursue.

Speaking the Truth Is the Best Way to Live

A foolish shepherd boy, as he tended his flock of sheep, cried out to the village people, "Wolf, wolf, wolf! There's a ferocious wolf!" The villagers ran in a flurry to assist the young boy, as he chuckled at them and said, "Ha, ha, ha, I was only kidding, there is no wolf."

After a month, the boy again screamed, "Help, help, there's a wolf! There's a wolf!" And when the villagers ran to the boy's aid, he laughed aloud at them . . . "There isn't any wolf, ha, ha, ha."

The village people were annoyed and very upset.

When he did it again the next month, just in case it was possibly true, they again came running at the boy's cries. Once again he mocked them.

Then one day, a large, fierce, ferocious wolf really did come to the field. The boy cried out in earnest . . . "Help me, help me, please, there is a wolf!" But this time no one came. The villagers ignored the boy's plea because they thought he was making up the story as he had done in the past. They paid no attention to the boy's desperate cries, and the wolf devoured the sheep.

The moral of this fable is that foolish people who habitually lie lose all respect and are not believed, even when they tell the truth.

We must live with total truth. When you are dishonest about even the little things, it makes people not trust you when it comes to the big things. Always tell the truth. Sir Walter Scott said, "Oh what a tangled web we weave, when first we practice to deceive." Lies are eventually exposed, so make life more peaceful and build respect for yourself with truth.

Many times we have been caught off-guard and have had to respond to something quickly. The right words will come out if we keep our determination to tell the truth habitually. Sometimes we receive stinging remarks from others, and it is like an ice-cold cup of water splashed in the face. I find it is best not to say anything when this happens and to be quiet and thoughtful for a moment. One of the characteristics of greatness is being able to endure contradictions without resentment and, if we must speak, to speak the truth in love.

There are genuinely good people in this world that you can rely on and count on, those who will respect your sincerity. Be fervent in truth and trust with the same intensity, and love will flourish.

What are the elements that build or rebuild trust? When there is a bond of faithfulness or a pledge to serve or love another, it must be totally unselfish. Love looks out for the best for others. Practice kindness and truthfulness. Listen to another's words carefully and watch their actions. Soon they will reveal whether they are trustworthy or not. If tempted to criticize, do it constructively, in respect and with honesty, and if they are mature, it will be effective. You can open your heart when you find an honest, trustworthy, and kind soul.

The most constructive criticism begins with praise, acknowledging the good points and suggesting how one can do even better. We always want to do better for those who respect us. This is a natural response. How good it is to know that we can choose to do right.

Life is noble when lived in the simplicity of the Word of God. "So put away lying, speak every man truth with his neighbor, for we are members one of another."—Ephesians 4:25.

God will bless you in truth, my dear readers.

The Song of Praise

The birds wake up at the break of day and sing a song of praise before they begin the necessary activities ahead.

They sing their melodies joyfully to God for the precious and glorious morning. And from their praise they gain virtue, power, and energy to face what lies ahead. For the joy of the Lord is their strength. Listen to the heavenly range of sounds, the jubilant orchestration, as the birds sing His praises.

We, too, must rejoice in what God has given to us so that we can have strength for the day. Begin now by saying, "Thank you," "Thank you for this . . . " and watch your mind, body, and spirit begin to lift. The more you praise Him, the higher you will soar, like the eagle far above all earthly cares and worries.

The power of the words of the enemy will lose their strength and become like the chatter of chipmunks on the ground.

God bathes the tiniest rose with dew and feeds the sparrows. Think of how much more value you are to Him and how much He loves you. Be grateful for the opportunity to be free to praise Him for the special person that you are.

A French proverb tells us that "gratitude creates the heart's memory." Begin to practice this beautiful principle in your life and watch miraculous joys unfold. Gratitude unleashes floods and torrents of happiness that turns what little we have into so much more, as you focus on the abundance of blessings that you have rather than the things that you may be lacking.

God will receive the praise you give with great joy and, in return, will fill your heart with happiness and strength. This is the true circle of life, so give and receive the very best.

Start a "praise" book. Each day, write down and express to God something for which you are thankful. Take inventory now of your life's treasures. "The first wealth is health," said Ralph Waldo Emerson. Express appreciation for your health, your family, a friend, or an acquaintance. Overflow with gratefulness.

Notice and give thanks for each day's gifts, big or small. The sight of a sunset, the laughter of a child, and hearing the words "I love you." Count your blessings one by one.

Praise Him who created you to be enthralled over a snowflake, twinkling stars, the warmth of home, and food on the table. Thankfulness can turn a simple dinner into a feast, a home into a castle, and an acquaintance into a beloved friend. Your heart will be awakened to the heralding trumpet of transforming power in praise.

Praise can be expressed in the form of helping those in need. After a kind and generous deed, ask the recipient to say aloud to God that evening "thank you," because you will be saying "thank you" to God for the joyful opportunity to help them. God will rejoice from above, as you appreciate all that He has given.

A surge of thankfulness comes again in the songs of the birds as they flutter to their nests in the dusk of the evening. End each day as the birds do, with a song of praise and a grateful heart expressing joy, peace, and harmony. You will receive a blessing of benediction, "For so He giveth His beloved sleep." "Sing to the Lord a new song, for He has done marvelous things."—Psalm 98:1.

Remember that God created a marvelous you to praise Him.

Doing Good Will Come Back to You

There was a story in Aesop's fables about the lion and the mouse. Reading this classic story to my little daughters enlightened us all.

A strong lion lay sleeping under a shady tree when a tiny mouse awakened him. The lion swiftly grabbed the little mouse with his giant paw and held him very tight. "Please, great lion," the mouse begged, "please let me go this one time and someday I'll help you."

The lion laughed to think that a teeny mouse could ever help a great king like himself, but in a moment of compassion, he let him go. "I won't ever forget your kindness, sir," the mouse said.

Months turned into years, and the lion forgot about the promise from the mouse.

In the jungle one morning, hunters set a net under some leaves, and it wasn't long before the mighty lion came wandering down the path, not suspecting anything.

The net caught the lion and his roar rang through the forest for someone to help him. The long-forgotten little mouse heard the lion's cries and went off immediately to help him. "I'm here, dear lion, I've come to set you free," the mouse exclaimed.

With his tiny, sharp teeth, the mouse gnawed through the ropes, saved the lion, and the lion escaped.

The moral of the story is one good turn deserves another. I think of the verse in the Bible, "Do to others what you would like them to do to you."

Aesop was a Greek storyteller, full of wisdom. And much of his wisdom is verified by biblical truths. Wisdom is wisdom, whether it is told in children's stories, the weighty tomes of philosophers, or parables in the Bible. To gain wisdom is of the utmost importance.

I have learned to not hesitate to be good, kind, and courteous to others. It will come back to you. One can never tell when, but it surely will. We all have our goals and desired achievements. The possibilities you have to succeed along the road of life are innumerable, but you must play fair.

Your personality is the sum of all your experiences, from your birth onward, and how you react to them. God put in each one of us an ability to impact each other's lives. Look for character in others.

My husband is now out in the yard pulling weeds so that our lawn will have lovely, smooth green grass. I think of his determination to do this even though it is a dirty, sweaty job. But whatever the cost, there is only one way to produce the luxury of a velvety green carpet, an ideal lawn. And so we have to be willing, whatever the cost, to pull out the thoughts that are the weeds in our mind, so that we can have a pure velvet peace.

Others can choose to be catty, resentful, and miserable. You can be whatever you want to be in your heart. If you are unhappy, dig down deep, and if there is something there that you are doing or thinking that is not really you, pull out those weeds and throw them in the trash.

Never underestimate the power of your thoughts and actions. With one small gesture you can help to change your life or that of another person. Remember William Penn's words, "I shall pass through this world only once. If therefore there's any kindness I can show or any good thing I can do let me do it now. Let me not defer or neglect it, for I shall not pass this way again."

When someone does a kind deed for me, I cherish it and I will forever remember his or her gentleness and kindness. God will remember it forever, too.

Part Two

BODY

"When health is absent, wisdom cannot reveal itself, art cannot become manifest, strength cannot be exerted, wealth is useless and reason is powerless."
—Herophilus, 300 B.C.

Forgiveness Is a Vital Quality

"I forgive you." These may be the three most important words you'll ever say. When you put wrongs behind you, your own life will be transformed.

Peter asked, "Lord, how many times shall I forgive my brother when he sins against me? Up to seven times?" He thought he was being more than generous, until he heard God's answer. "I tell you," the Lord said, "not seven times, but seventy times seven."—Matthew 18:21–22.

We can completely destroy the ability of the enemy to hurt us through any person by completely and totally forgiving them... as we want God to forgive us.

Be the first to forgive a wrongdoing. Forgiveness is freedom and important to our own eternal happiness. Without it, life is governed by an endless cycle of resentment and retaliation.

"In suffering, one learns many things . . . that it is important not to be responsible for deliberately bringing pain into the lives of others . . . that without a willingness to forgive those who hurt us, it is not likely that our lives can go on in a meaningful manner."—Charles Dickens.

To forgive is characteristic of strength. Gandhi reminded us that "Forgiveness is the virtue of the brave." It is the key to deliverance, personal peace, and contentment. It consoles and heals not just one person, but all involved. Letting go of a grudge can be one of the best things you can do for your health. Forgiveness is as good for the body as it is for the soul.

Several studies have found that worrying about a wrongdoing has been linked to several health problems, ranging from headaches to heart attacks. A deep-seated grudge can eat away at your peace of mind. Nursing a grievance, the kind that you harbor inside, can cause it to fester and harm your well-being. By forgiving, you short-circuit anger's poisonous power. So begin now to let go of hostility, bitterness, and wrath. Replace it with a new beginning and a clean slate. I read that the Bible says, "Forgive us our trespasses . . . as we forgive those who trespass against us." Defined in the American Heritage Dictionary, "as" means "to the same extent or degree; equally." Therefore, if we want to be forgiven, we must ask God to grant us the grace to forgive others, as we want God to forgive us.

Forgiveness is a choice freely made. It is a gift we can give or withhold. And when it is offered to us, we can accept it or reject it. We can be free or remain in bondage.

There are occasions when we all need to be forgiven. Remember the times you have been forgiven of your faults. How good it is to be trusted again. This may help you be more tolerant of others.

Realize that people make mistakes, and try to accept their shortcomings. Focus on and look for the individual's good qualities.

Step into the other person's shoes. Try to understand, from their point of view, what makes him or her do the things that make you angry. Communicate the problem. Express your concern calmly and honestly with the person involved. Then look ahead to a clear, bright future, and don't bring the situation up again. God has a sea of forgiveness into which He throws all of our sins when we confess them. On the shore of that sea is a sign that says, "No fishing." Forgive and forget.

Forgiveness shows that divine spark within us, for it is love. It is an act of faith born out of concern for the well-being of others stemming from God's love for us. To forgive is one of the highest and most beautiful forms of love. Do not wait to forgive, for by forgiving, you become the master of your fate and the doer of miracles.

The Prescription for a Long Life

It was a joyful celebration for a dear man's ninetieth birthday. A reporter from the local newspaper attended the event and asked the man, "Sir, your wife said that you have never been sick a day in your life and you have never been to a doctor . . . is that a fact?" The man replied with a twinkle in his eye, "That's not entirely so. The reason I've never been sick is I have the two best doctors in the world, Dr. Walking and Dr. Laughter."

Our bodies are amazing machines. With our hearts beating an average of 100,000 times a day, we have been beautifully and wonderfully made.

I know the Bible says that laughter is medicine to our bones. Now that is the truth. Do you have arthritis, osteoporosis, or any bone problem? Take this prescription from Dr. Laughter, three times a day with meals, and watch the amazing results. A sense of humor about every situation tinged with love can take the cutting edge off of every trial. Doctors say the healing rate is two times faster for patients who faithfully take this prescribed medicine.

Do you think you don't have time to walk? Well, exercise does not take time out of your life; it puts life into your time. Schedule your walk on your calendar and adhere to it without excuse. It won't happen by accident, so try to set aside a few minutes each day to exercise. Even ten minutes a few times a day can make a difference.

Go window-shopping, visit the park with the family, or suggest going for a walk with a friend. Climb up and down the stairs a few times at home, pedal a stationary bike while watching a video, do sit-ups as the children build with Lego blocks on the floor. It will mean so much that you are there with them. Be creative and versatile with your exercise routine.

Aerobic activity can help you build endurance, reduce body fat, and improve your self-esteem. Choose an activity you enjoy and stick with it. Swimming, aerobic dance, and walking help to bring oxygen to your brain and diminish depression.

Try exercise machines for the convenience of working out indoors. I have a friend who picked up a perfectly good exercise bike off the sidewalk as someone was throwing it away. You can get exercise equipment for practically nothing at tag sales. Why? Because it is hard to adopt new habits. But with persistence, you can do it.

Aim for three twenty-minute sessions every week and slowly increase the duration. Always check with your doctor before beginning any exercise program.

Combine aerobics with strength training for a well-rounded routine as you become increasingly able. You will not only get fit but excited with the beginning of "A New You." Then, start eating more fruits, vegetables, and fish and less red meat and the wrong kinds of fats. Use extra virgin olive oil in place of butter and other oils.

To reduce stress and frustration, don't forget to nourish your inner being. Do something special for yourself—gather one favorite scripture to your heart daily. Memorize it as you sit quietly with a cup of tea.

Tune in to music you enjoy or that has special significance to you. Research shows that music therapy is an effective way to reduce stress. Listen to the Great Composer of the symphony of life and enjoy it. This unhurried time will do wonders for your mind, body, and soul.

Remember to take the best medicine, which is preventive medicine. It costs nothing, prescribed only by Dr. Walking and Dr. Laughter— which is the joy of life appreciated and savored in all its beauty.

Make Time for Things That Count

As Thoreau once wrote, "If I shall sell both my forenoons and afternoons to society, as most appear to do, I am sure that for me there would be nothing left worth living for."

There never seems to be enough time. Minutes melt into hours, days into weeks, and months into years, so suddenly, so swiftly. Time, a most precious jewel, a priceless commodity, is our most fleeting possession.

Today, we all need to make a conscious effort to make time for the things that really count: communion with God and with your spouse, a walk by the shore, sincere fellowship between friends, nestling in a comfy chair reading a good book, saying "I'm sorry," and encouraging a child. These things alone will give you a full and meaningful life.

In this busy world of constant activity, separate yourself from the countless demands, stress, and strain of the work world. Get to a quiet place in your home or yard to be calm, to meditate on God's wisdom. Silence is essential for healing our nerves and letting God's peace saturate our souls. Create a safe haven, a place to rest, read, and pray.

At first, everything you need to get done will invade your mind and try to get you to give up your special time of serenity. However, you must set aside occasions to renew your own spirit. Make time to eat quietly, sleep well, and take good care of yourself so that you can care for others. Establish a plan that works for you. Quiet meditation first, then perhaps a walk. Let an allotment of your day be for your own personal pleasure.

I remember the story of a man who was about to die. What he said he valued most in his life were not the awards he won at work, the long hours he spent at the office, or the size of his bank account, but his great treasures: his children, his devoted wife, the lawn he loved to mow, and the hiking trails he and his family explored. Think for a moment: What is most important to you?

Make time to witness the enchanting gifts of the season: Hear the droplets of the silver rain as they tap on your window, smell the floral-perfumed breezes, and see the hills layered in green. Nature's beauty, intertwined with our praises, glorifies the wondrous things that God can do.

It only takes a moment to thank God for the many blessings that decorate our days, or to say a prayer for someone who has a special need, or to share the joy of the Lord in your heart with someone you love. Spreading sunshine and doing good deeds will come back to you many times over.

If you want peace with God, take time to get to know Him and He will give you the strength and inspiration for all else you need to do in life. That word "need" can simplify life exceedingly.

I read in the Scriptures, "My God will supply all our needs." Not our wants, but our needs. You may want a palace, but you need just a little private space to call your own where you can meet quietly with Him. He will supply that bit of treasured time.

I like to remember in His Word He said, "I'll never leave you or forsake you." So no matter what changes may take place in my life, I know God is holding my hand.

When we are holding His hand, I believe we step out of time and into a bit of eternity where everything is perfect and all solutions become clear.

Let your body be calm as you bask in sweet tranquility. For one of the greatest gifts of all is God's timeless eternity filled with the love and comfort He gives.

After Fifteen Minutes of Walking, You Feel Great

I know the Lord loves an even balance. So years ago, I started taking notes on diet secrets. One of the best I ever heard was don't eat anything while standing up. That's right—no snacking while standing by the refrigerator, eating on the run, or sampling food while cooking dinner. Sit down, eat slowly, savor your meal, and make it an event.

Also, I've read about the fifteen-minute rule, which means you wait fifteen minutes before eating something you crave. What usually transpires is that within fifteen minutes, something happens to take your mind off food.

As for exercising, when you just don't want to work out, say to yourself, "I will do some sort of activity for fifteen minutes and then stop." Most often you start to feel so good that you continue.

I know that when I make time to exercise, I feel more energetic, happier, and eager to face the world.

Finding the time for physical activity is most people's biggest challenge. Try waking up a half-hour earlier to exercise. Watching a fitness show, putting on a workout video, or simply doing sit-ups, and leg lifts will start your day off right. Park in the farthest parking spot and walk to the mall. Walk instead of driving to do your errands. If possible, walk to the post office or the cleaners. Enjoy a stroll to the park or on the beach. You'll feel so good after a twenty-minute workout that you'll want to enlist a friend and exercise together. It's a great way to keep up the good habit.

Bike to a destination. Europeans are way ahead of us in this respect. Take a brisk walk with your spouse after work. It will be a good chance for the two of you to talk about your day.

- Subtle lifestyle changes can keep weight off because you are more likely to stick with them. Each week introduce one new fruit or vegetable into your menu and let it replace a starch or fat.
- To keep your energy level up, bring healthful foods with you to the office: fruit, almonds, yogurt, or low-carbohydrate energy bars.
- When dining out, remember you have choices. Before you go to the restaurant, decide what you will eat to avoid temptation. Ask the waiter not to bring the bread and butter. Have an appetizer and salad only and request a simple dressing of olive oil and fresh lemon. Focus on food preparation and portion control.
- Use smaller plates to make modest portions look larger. Try having at least three colorful vegetables on your plate, thereby satisfying your esthetic visual sense.
- Drench your appetite. Water can tame your cravings; it helps to fill up your stomach and takes away hunger pains. We need to drink eight to ten glasses of water daily to be properly hydrated.
- Consult with your doctor before beginning any diet/exercise plan.
- Give yourself a pep talk. When you need a bit of encouragement, know that every small step is a major masterpiece. Take pride in your accomplishments and act as if you have already met your goal.

Keep a pride list of your past successes and read it often.

1. "I started."
2. "I'm still determined."
3. "I lost two pounds."
4. "A five-pound victory luncheon with friends."

Let me close this essay with a Native American prayer:

"And the wind said, 'May you be as strong as the oak, yet flexible as the birch; may you stand tall as the redwood and live gracefully as the willow; and may you always bear fruit all your days on this earth.'"

Find the Time for the Joy of Inner Peace

In gardens of quiet beauty, there are wavelets of tranquility and mysterious sanctuaries that harbor the symphonies of nature. We can also find the place within our soul that is serene and still. Here is where we can listen to the music of our heart and follow where it leads. Find the door to your secret garden and open it.

Think back as far as you can to the time in your childhood when you laid on the grass and studied the clouds and heard the birds sing their praise; when you looked up into a starry night and thought of God. There you can renew the awareness of your soul and be transformed in your spirit. Rest in this inner peace, in the inviolable security that comes with God's presence.

This is not an experience restricted to childhood alone. It is the touch of divine providence to get your attention before the enemy of our soul sticks his cloven hoof in the door. His tactic is the opposite of peace. His world becomes a frantic place where no one is satisfied, where thievery is the norm and lying the excuse. It is a world that urges us to take on the stress and strain of greed and climbing up the social and corporate ladder. We find that these goals are empty and disappointing—yet they are all-consuming, never leaving us enough time to pause for a breath.

The enemy's words are hurry, hurry, hurry. Remember that he is like the basketball guard with arms waving. The enemy doesn't want to see you relaxed and tapping into the reality of inner peace and beauty. But it is possible to do so if only we make ourselves sit still and look and listen for Him.

I love the verse in the Bible that says, "In quietness and confidence shall be your strength." In that quietness, feel the presence of God. There is nothing better than that. It is the greatest joy in the entire world, greater than possessing all the planets in the solar system, the stars, or the riches of royal treasure.

We all know the dissatisfaction in the lives of some of the rich and famous, those who failed to find happiness or even simple contentment in their wealth and vast domains. However, those who are wise found it in the awesome and pure love of God. Let us commit our homes, our lives, and our minds to Him. He will give us peace.

Have we done the much-needed spring cleaning of our minds? Tell your Heavenly Father you are sorry you have looked to everything else but Him. And when you are stilled, hear what He will reveal to you. God will guide your thoughts and actions aright and express to you your higher self in every circumstance.

If God says, "Check, check, check," check your attitude, objectives, and motives. You can rest in the fact that He is all-knowing and all-wise. No matter how others react—family, friends, or business associates—we can be, by relaxing in Him, the very best contribution to this world we can possibly be.

Listen to His still, small voice of direction. Looking inward to self alone will just drive depression deeper. Invite God to take permanent residence in your heart. He will show you there is no other way to happiness than by giving outwardly to others. I love the saying, "There is no greater exercise for the heart than to reach down and pick up another."

Look around you; find someone to encourage and speak kindly to. Then at the end of the day, retreat to that little room in the heart where you will find the open arms of God, who welcomes you to the rest and sanctuary of your soul.

Smile As the Light from Within Shines Bright

Mark Twain once said, "Wrinkles should merely indicate where smiles have been."

Did you know it takes twenty-six muscles to smile and sixty-two muscles to frown? So what are you waiting for? Always be smiling.

In life, real joy is not in the possession of things; it is found in a thankful heart. Our own heart is the witness; it's not the opinions of others that forms our true honor. Conduct yourself in such a way that you'll have no regrets. Hold yourself to a high standard and the highest reward will be yours. We can create joy by living fully and living right.

A happy heart is the best service we can give to God. Smile and your burdens will be lighter; smile and your outlook will be kinder. Summon your sense of humor and gain strength. Humor is a wonderful tool to bring things into perspective. A good laugh can transform tears into contentment and is a great stress reliever. Laugh your troubles away by keeping funny videos or books on hand. Try collecting funny pictures or cartoons in a scrapbook to chase away the blues on a dreary day.

Be around children; they are a breath of fresh air, and their laughter is infectious. A sense of humor reduces people and problems to their right proportions.

It is so easy today, with all the media reporting the tragic, to get your mind and body off balance. Then depression sets in. We must strive to keep an even balance. So just be determined to not let stress overwhelm you.

Develop healthy coping skills. Talking things over with friends and talking things over with God are good antidotes to stress.

Try listing all the things in your life you appreciate. This will unstress you quickly, and thankfulness will adjust your attitude. See stress as a challenge and see yourself in charge of it. If you refuse to be overpowered by stress, you won't suffer unhealthy side effects. Stress hurts immunity and taxes the body, so give the tensions and strains to God and purposely relax as you do your best.

How many times has a man chosen a plainer, calmer woman over a glamorous yet stressed and wired one? I read in 1 Peter 3:4 that it says, "Let your adornment be the unfading beauty of a gentle and quiet spirit." It is of greater worth than all the glamour in the world. It's more important to be beautiful on the inside than on the outside. In the long haul, that peaceful sweetness lingers on and creates a prevailing beauty that permeates the heart. By smiling, you light the candle of your soul.

"I wake up in the morning and have two choices, to be grumpy or to be cheerful," wrote a seventy-year-old Massachusetts resident. "I don't have much to offer in material things, but God gave me a smile and I use that. Plus, if you have the Lord, you have everything. I ask Him for His divine love and will in my life. If you have God on your side, you have everything." Can you imagine how the world would be if we all thought that way and were content to do just that?

Mornings are one of my favorite times of the day, when everything is so fresh and clean and the earth has renewed itself. Today, I will rejoice that I am alive, and that rain or shine, I have the privilege to do all I can to help others have something to smile about!

Our Beautiful Individuality Counts Most

*B*ehold the stars in the heavens, a vast array of them. God made every one and He sits in the midst of it all, looking down upon us. The mountainside is dotted with lush green grasses, and flowers fill the forests, draping the land anew in beauty.

Deer graze and the squirrels chatter as the birds sing and wing their way to nest building. In the sunlight, on the trees, in the air, and on the land are a myriad of butterflies and delightful chirping insects, as far as the eye can see.

And still further, in all that vast quantity, are people made in the image of God. Not one the same, not even one fingerprint the same. There is only one of you, a one-of-a-kind person, unique in the entire world.

As I tell my daughters, "You were in God's thoughts before the foundation of the world. He put a bit of Himself in you to lead and guide you to bring out in you the beauty of His thoughts." We must realize now what a jewel we are. God didn't make us as a string of paper dolls. You are one of a kind, created to express Him.

Have you ever felt like you don't fit in with the crowd? Are you called the oddball? Have others made fun of you? Well, do not fret. Walk tall and hold your head up high, because I'm here to reveal to you that it's an honor to be different.

Pay no mind to scorn or snobbery. It is not what others think of us that counts; it is what we think of ourselves. Sometimes we have to let others play their little games. They join forces and think that there will be no retribution, but my Heavenly Father has told me, "As they have treated others, they too will be treated." Don't waste your energy worrying about things that might happen or about other people's opinions. God gave each one of us different talents to express the unique gifts within us. Some can write, some can sing, some can paint, build, or repair and make things right again. Some have the wonderful gift of compassion and understanding. They open their hearts and welcome others. What beautiful gifts those are.

A Connecticut resident said, "When someone rushes to open a door for me or asks me if I need any help, I always say, 'Thank You, Lord. I just knew You would send Your angel to help me.' For there are angels out there in this world."

A touch from God can reveal your gift to you. I can tell you from experience that when I am with a friend that is like-minded, we seem to be aware of the fact that there is always one more among us. Thee and me and God make three. That knowledge and joy cannot help but spill over to others and draw them like bees to honey.

I know that when Jesus prayed in John 17, He said, "That they all may be one as thou Father are in me and I in thee, that they also may be one in us."

This assures me that I am never alone and this is the only example I cling to, to be like another. I want to be one with Him and my friends who are in Him.

Here is the promise that binds our hearts together. Though we may be thousands of miles apart, I rejoice that as you read this essay, you agree in heart that we are different . . . but we are one.

Health Is Wealth

The phone rang at 3:37 A.M. Though it was the middle of the night, I was not alarmed. Our close friends, Dave and Melissa, were expecting a new baby any day.

An elated male voice at the other end of the phone said, "We're at the hospital!"

"Did she have the baby?" I groggily asked. "Yes," he said. And before I could ask if it was a boy or girl, he exclaimed with humble thankfulness, "It's healthy!"

Your health, your well-being, is your treasure from God. I know the Bible says, "The body is the temple of the Holy Spirit." So we must respect it as our dwelling place.

How many times do we take this priceless commodity for granted? It is only when we are faced with sickness or pain that we realize that the old saying is true: "If you have your health, you have just about everything." Respect what God has given you and take care of the beautiful wrapping of your soul.

Exercise regularly for better health. Walking briskly for ten minutes a day can help prevent heart disease, high blood pressure, diabetes, and some forms of cancer concluded experts from the Centers for Disease Control and Prevention and the American College of Sports Medicine. Walk to the library instead of driving, walk around the block with the family before dinner, or drive to the park and walk a couple of times around it.

Balanced food is health. You wouldn't only put gasoline into your car; it must have oil, too. Eat your fruits and vegetables along with the meat and potatoes.

Keep stress out! In two words: simplify, simplify. When you unclutter your life, you clear your mind of stress and strain. Say a prayer, breathe deeply, open the curtains, and let the sunshine stream in. Light can activate endorphins, which are chemicals that make you feel happy. Engage in hearty laughter. According to one study, when we laugh the body suppresses its production of stress hormones, alleviating depression.

The joy of seeing the results of helping others is priceless. Do a good deed in secret and reap a joy-filled countenance outwardly. Help a neighbor in need or take a treat to a shut-in.

Have quiet time each day for rest and renewal. It is soothing for your spirit to just relax. Find the joy in all that you do. Have creative outlets; spend time with people who make you happy and make you feel better about yourself. Be content with whatever you have. A thankful heart can put everything in perspective.

Choose very, very carefully the words that come out of your mouth. I've so often wondered, what if God said, "From this day forward, you can have exactly what you say."

Words are creative, and you set the atmosphere in your house. Let it be one of encouragement and peace.

Keep a book of uplifting thoughts by your bedside table. Inspiring messages before bedtime can heal your body while you sleep. Round out every day with essential nourishment of love, peace, quiet, and forgiveness.

Develop a success-expectant attitude, because you'll most often get what you expect. There is power in believing. What you expect and believe in your heart can come to pass. Take good care of yourself, live to the fullest, and awaken your passion for life. Be all that you want to be. Dream impossible dreams and then go out and achieve them!

What a wonderful paradox that can be!

Create Heaven on Earth in Your Home

As I read in Joshua 24:15, "Choose you this day whom you shall serve. As for me and my house we will serve the Lord." We have a choice as to what we make our dwelling places to be.

A home should be like a heaven on earth, an oasis, a peaceful place. It is so important to guard what comes into your home and to secure its refreshing atmosphere. Make your home a very exclusive place wherein only the finest things of life can enter, choosing your friends with wisdom, your music and entertainment with discretion.

When God is in your heart, love is in your home. "The Lord blesses the home of the righteous."—Proverbs 3:33.

Let love fill every room of your home. Pray together and build strong family bonds. Provide an atmosphere of love and the awareness of God's presence. Cultivate an ongoing consciousness that the Lord is the head of the house and is upholding all of you in His everlasting arms.

Handle your home life and the raising of your children with great wisdom. Your example and influence is the foundation of their lives. Sometimes we are so eager to give our kids what we never had, we forget to give them what we did have. Virtues like honesty, kindness, compassion, and courage will do more for a child than a full bank account or designer clothes. Security, confidence, self-esteem, and a faith in God are some of the most important traits for youngsters to grasp in order to be a contented and secure adult. It takes work to bring up a child right. You are the master sculptor, creating an image of great beauty.

Surround your family with things you know will benefit them. Parents are teachers. Open the gates of your children's minds by sharing poetry and reading the Bible together. Broaden their horizons by introducing them to classical music. Create joyous moments, making lasting memories that will be carried on for generations.

Do not expose yourself to negative news. The more we expose ourselves to negative things in this world, the more we sap our own energy. Therefore we must strive to create beauty, loveliness, and order for others and ourselves. Nervousness and irritations drop away when things are in place. Keep things in order. Enjoy the wonderful satisfaction of accomplishment as you straighten out the closets and drawers and eliminate clutter while listening to Bach. Play peaceful music throughout your home. Beautiful music can inspire and motivate.

Inspire with meaningful décor, such as encouraging scriptural verses in charming gold frames.

Outdoors, plant beautiful flowers along your walkway to welcome guests. Hang a basket of lovely blossoms on the porch or fill an urn with colorful pansies. Bring the outdoors in with a bouquet of fresh flowers for the table. Flowers have a wonderful way of showing us God's miraculous beauty while reminding us of His love. These things have a way of remaining in our hearts and being long remembered.

A fragrant home is a place of sweet repose. Set bowls of potpourri around your home. Scented candles can bring romance to the setting. The aroma of apple pie baking, a roast in the oven, or grandma's pasta sauce can warm the heart and bring back childhood memories.

When we stop and give praise and thanks to God, every molecule of our body comes to rest and is revived. So keep your hearts filled with God and let His love be the crowning glory in your home. Focus on His Word and give your cares to He who said, "Cast all your cares upon me for I care for you." Pursue the high and holy calling of creating a happy home. It is so true, "Be it ever so humble, there is no place like home."

When You Live Right, You Live Longer

I've heard it said that you are as young as your faith, as old as your doubt; as young as your self-confidence, as old as your fear; as young as your hope and as old as your despair. Age is just an outward manifestation of how much wisdom is contained within.

One centenarian attributed her long life to God's plan. "He has a special plan for each of us and He is not quite done with me yet," she states at age 104. "Grey hair is a crown of glory, if it is accompanied by a righteous life."—Proverbs 16:31.

According to research, those who live to a healthy 100 nearly always profess a strong faith in God. Also, strong religious faith is associated with a higher self-esteem, less anxiety, and lower rates of depression.

Next to faith in God, the most valuable attributes we can acquire are love for our fellow man and a good sense of humor. We have to remember that the Lord loves an even balance. It is important to Him that we take care of our body, which is His chosen place of earthly dwelling. Mind, body, and spirit—these three in proportion represent an even balance. Here are some ways to help achieve that balance:

- Start the day with prayer and appreciation, and read at least one verse of God's Word. Each day should be utilized to the fullest. It is God's gift to us, and what we do with it is our gift to God.
- Eat a healthy breakfast. Some nutritious choices include whole-grain cereal, whole-wheat bread, yogurt, and fresh fruit. If you don't have time in the morning, plan ahead. Set the breakfast table in the evening and put your daily devotional book beside your place mat.

- Have at least five servings a day of fruits and vegetables. You'll get the biggest health boost from dark green, orange, and red varieties. Eat more fish. Studies show that eating three servings each week will reduce your risk of a heart attack by half.
- Some of the foods for longevity are tomatoes, olive oil, red grapes, nuts, whole grains, salmon, blueberries, garlic, spinach, and tea.
- Do not smoke. Numerous studies have linked smoking with osteoporosis, among other diseases. Avoid alcohol. Drinking can cause damage to the brain, as well as cause other ailments.
- Take vitamins. Lack of key nutrients, such as vitamin B, can promote dementia in the elderly. Some studies report that dementia can be reversed with proper diet and vitamin supplements.
- Considering your chosen vocation, the Bible says, "Whatsoever you do in word or deed, do it as unto the Lord." So do your work in all sincerity and with all your heart.
- When you come home, open your arms wide to receive the love that only your family can give. For those who live alone, the joy of a pet greeting you is so wonderful. Doctors say that people who own pets live longer, so get a pet if you can.
- Walk for an hour a day, and on cold days take your stroll through a shopping mall. Even twenty minutes, three times a week, is helpful, but always consult with your doctor.
- Increase your life span with social support. A network of friends can keep you active and enrich your life.
- Try to get enough sleep. Studies show that not getting enough rest can accelerate aging. A warm bath can help you relax after a hectic day, and praying until you fall asleep assures the companionship of angels through the night.

"May the Lord bless you . . . all the days of your life . . . "—Psalm 128:5.

God's Grace Can Be Found in His Silence

Shhh ... do you hear it? Not a sound ... peace and quiet. There is nothing like it—just the echoes of the gentle wind, the descending jewels of the sunset, and the hush of newly fallen snow.

It is then, in the still of silence, that I can hear the soft, small voice within my soul say, "I am your great reward." And I lift my eyes to the Heavens and behold His vast greatness.

I read in the Bible, "The wisdom of God is first peaceable." So find tranquility and contentment in productive quietness.

When the stress and strain that sometimes overwhelms us come, calm your heart by turning everything over to God. Go slow, take one day at a time, and find comfort in His Word, which says, "As your day is, so shall your strength be." God is sufficient for each day.

Why worry about tomorrow or past mistakes or failures? Why waste life's precious moments on anxiety?

Look at the sweet little birds. They have no hands to plant a garden or prepare food, yet God feeds them. The birds do not have a wool coat to keep their tiny bodies warm from the winter's chill. It amazes me that in a little body, God strikes up a furnace to keep them warm in the cold and ice. He supplies their needs. That is why we see sparrows in the winter. God let them be here as a testimony for those who are wise enough to see it. God takes care of His own. Remember that the Bible says, "You are of much more value than the sparrows." The birds do not worry. Trust in God, too, and find that He will care for you.

Let your life claim this tranquility of peace as you enjoy the beauty of creation, the mathematical perfection and the order that maintains the balance of the universe. Everything has God's fingerprints on it. See God in a beautiful sapphire-blue sky, in the eyes of a child, and the heart of a rose.

Nourish your soul, feed your spirit, and enlarge the greatness in your heart by partaking in things that give your life meaning and depth.

Begin your day gently. Morning rituals such as eating breakfast while reading a daily devotional book or the Bible can make you feel great the entire day. Following a routine like this can build tremendous strength of character.

Have daily quiet time. I love God's Word that says, "In quietness and confidence will be my strength." True contentment and strength comes from the Lord. Be still for a half hour. Rest, meditate, pray, and honor Him.

Listen to beautiful music. Experts in the field of music recommend using music as a tool to refresh life. Be stirred by the symphony, lifted by a gospel choir, and rejuvenated by the sounds of Vivaldi.

Sing joyfully the praises of God, for music was created to soothe the soul. Music has a healing power. Let its calming influence strengthen your immune system, eliminate stress, and become more relaxed.

Keep things in order. We've all heard the saying, "Cleanliness is next to godliness." When my house is clean and in order and my office organized, my mind functions better, and my soul is at rest. I know the Bible says, "Even the footsteps of the righteous are ordered by the Lord." He is in control when you turn the controls over to Him. Cast all your cares upon Him for He careth for you. Rest in that, dear reader.

You Are God's Well-Made Handiwork

You are wonderfully made. God's fingerprints are on you. Made in God's own image, you are so precious and valuable in His sight. We must take care of this wonderful mechanism, the body of your soul.

Approach a diet and exercise program from a health issue, not as a quest for a superficial image. For the fountain of true beauty comes from the heart, not the cosmetic counter.

"Let your adornment be the inner self with the lasting beauty of a gentle and quiet spirit which is very precious in God's sight."—Peter 3:4.

Ask any good mechanic how to care for a vehicle and he will tell you to change the oil every three thousand miles, replace the filters and spark plugs, and buy quality gasoline. Therefore, to take care of our own physical vehicles, we must consume nutritious foods to feel our very best. We must drink pure water, eat green vegetables and lots of fruit. Don't put fast food in your tank all the time!

To get an accurate sense of how much you eat, keep food diaries. Write down what you eat and at what times. Measure foods. Don't forget to count the mayonnaise in the tuna or the dressing on your salad. Use light or low-fat foods whenever possible. You'll have a better chance of sticking to a weight-loss plan if you choose to eat low-calorie foods you enjoy.

An Irish proverb says, "A good laugh and a long sleep are the best cures in the doctor's book." Get enough rest. People who don't get enough sleep are more likely to consume sugary and fatty foods just to get energy. Replace the candy bars with granola bars, and remember that a sense of humor can revitalize and give you a burst of vigor.

If you feel stress or boredom, you may be tempted to overeat. Try to divert that temptation. Do an art project, call a friend, or hit a tennis ball. Thirst can also mask itself as hunger. Drink at least eight 8-ounce glasses of water a day to be well hydrated and digest food efficiently.

Exercise is one of the best antidotes for depression. It increases metabolism, reduces stress, and elevates your mood. Movement affects your attitude. Once you start moving, blood starts to flow and you feel better. Studies show that people who exercise in the morning are more likely to stick with it than those who wait until evening, when they're too tired to work out. So schedule that workout as you would a business appointment, and stick to it.

Binges usually involve food that's readily available, so rid your cabinets of easy-access, high-calorie food. Keep a package of baby carrots and cut-up celery in the refrigerator for when you get the urge for something crunchy. Eliminate "unconscious" eating. Make a conscious effort to reform your food choices.

Chew gum while cooking dinner so you won't be tempted to sample the food while preparing it. Tasting food can add up to a whole meal.

Get plenty of nature's desserts. According to the U.S. Department of Agriculture, blueberries have the most health-promoting antioxidants. The next best are strawberries, plums, oranges, red grapes, kiwi, pink grapefruit, bananas, apples, pears, and honeydew melons. Prepare a bowl of these delicious fruits for a visual treat, and enjoy.

Before you go off to work, center yourself in God's will for the day. Retreat to a quiet place, if only for a moment, where you can entirely relax and put yourself in His care. All fears, doubts, and worries will disappear as you start the day full of confidence. Believe in yourself. You have the power to achieve your dreams.

Take good care of yourself, for you are wonderfully made . . . and I care that you care about yourself.

We All Must Take a Few Moments to Relax

In the Garden of Eden at dusk, when the whole world was soft and still in shades of mother-of-pearl, God came down and talked with Adam and Eve.

In the cool of the evening He asked, "My darling children, how was your day in this paradise that I created for you to enjoy?" God sat with them and they communed together in a serene, sacred, and quiet joy.

Adam and Eve delighted in the beautiful pattern of life that God designed for them, quieted their spirits, and laid down their bodies in sweet repose.

We have been created to take quiet moments at the end of the day to just sit, relax, and think on the loveliness of God. Sometimes we get so stressed and tired that we can't even think straight. Let us go back to Eden's example and start anew a very old pattern of peacefulness.

Balance in our lives is crucial. We all know we rush and hurry, but what about the tranquil, thankful times? Have we left those out of our lives?

We have but one life; we must do the things that can create in us appreciation, love, and rest. God's pure grace and His remarkable wonders can be found by sitting alone at a local beach, hearing the sounds of the waves crashing, and feeling the ocean's breeze.

If you enjoy peaceful music, then make the time to listen to it.

There is a beautiful old hymn that says, "Shut in with God in a secret place, there in the spirit beholding His face. Gaining new power to run in the race, I love to be shut in with God." Sometimes "shut in" should be synonymous with "shut off." Shut off the television, the radio, the car motor, the telephone, and the computer . . . and give a big sigh of relief. What a great joy and strength-giver is peace. The nerves heal, the inspiration comes, and ideas for creativity flow.

It has been the experience of many that if you give up the day's problems to God at night, He can speak to your subconscious while you sleep, so that with the dawn's shining light comes the solution. Why not try it? Make your requests known to God with thanksgiving, and simplify your life by taking this method to unwind.

I must have time to unwind. After a busy day at the office, hurrying to pick up the baby, sitting in traffic, rushing to prepare dinner, putting in a load of laundry, washing the dishes, cleaning the kitchen, we all get so tired. Then it's time to bathe the children, try to get them to sleep by eight or nine, make lunches for the next day, read the mail, and so on and so on.

By then, I am really exhausted. I sit down, fold the clothes, glance at the newspaper, and talk with my husband. Before I go to sleep I must have quiet time to unwind, shut in with God, to gain a moment of refreshing strength to sleep in all through the night. We all need this time for renewal. Let's not live life so fast that we leave out what is so important.

"The Lord will give strength to his people; the Lord will bless his people with peace." —Psalm 29:11.

Breathe sighs of contentment as you talk to God, read poetry, write in your journal, or simply relish the serene beauty of a velvety sky scattered with stars. Let the soothing balm of the Lord's gentle spirit wash over you as you find yourself relaxed so you can sleep soundly in the arms of your Heavenly Father.

Humor Enriches Our Lives and Lessens Burdens

Humor is one of God's marvelous gifts. Humor gives us smiles, laughter, and fun. It reveals the roses and helps to hide the thorns. It softens the harshness of life for you and for others. Humor makes our heavy burdens light, smoothes the rough spots in our paths, and eases the tension in our heavy workloads. A Chinese proverb tells us that "Happiness never decreases by being shared." So share the gift of a wonderful and hearty sense of humor with someone else.

Studies show that laughter reduces pain and increases alertness and energy. It can be a powerful antidote to stress. When you smile, your facial muscles press against nerves that release chemicals in the brain that give you a sense of well-being. Doctors find that laughter seems to promote the healing of the body. And I know God's Word says, "A merry heart doeth good like a medicine."

If you feel you have lost your sense of humor, ask God for one and He will gladly give it to you. His Word says it is for your own good. So begin to look for that sense of humor to pop up in all aspects of your life. Forget the mistakes of the past; God loves you.

Remember the old saying, "Laugh and the world will laugh with you." A friend once told me that when she was in elementary school, her mother wrote in her autograph book a verse that she would always recall. It read, "The world is like a mirror, reflecting what you do, and if you face it smiling, it smiles right back at you."

Find time to relax and watch the squirrels at their play, and keep the enemy from blowing fears out of proportion. Humor helps to keep things in perspective, and a sense of humor can help us smooth over disappointments and adversities. It's the delightful balm that can turn your difficulty into a source of strength. "You will have pain, but your pain will turn to joy."—John 16:20.

People who look at the lighter side of life are less often depressed and bounce back quicker from sad events. They tend to have better health and may even live longer. They lift their mind above life's little irritations and keep their cool. Keep your emotions in balance, and do not let petty things annoy or disturb you.

Make the best of every situation and never lose your ability to laugh at yourself and at life.

If a situation is troubling you, share it with a trusted friend once and put it in God's hands. Try not to talk about it over and over again. If you don't keep rehashing the circumstances in your mind, eventually its effect on you will lose its power and fade away.

Your joy will return quickly as you brighten up your day by doing something kind and unexpected for someone who is feeling down. Maybe you can clip a cartoon from the newspaper and send it to a friend. Smile and nod a "hello" to everyone you see. Send a warm thank-you note to a person who has enriched your life. Enjoy the companionship of loved ones and friends. Laughter can spark creativity, so inject humor into your business environment in memos or meetings. Bring good cheer wherever you go, and find happiness in the simple things of life. Count your blessings and thank God for giving you another precious day.

Soon you will be able to sing, as did the psalmist, "You have turned my mourning into dancing and clothed me with joy."—Psalm 30:11.

Have a happy heart, dear ones.

Let Children Know You Believe in Them

*E*very child is a success waiting to begin. When John the Baptist was born, his father sang a beautiful song about all the things his son would do. He would be a prophet and prepare the way for the Lord.

The father instilled confidence, love, and great faith in the boy, who achieved all that his father imagined . . . and more.

It is a glorious thing when people believe in you. How much this means to little children. Support your child's dreams, hopes, and aspirations. Every child is a unique masterpiece, with individual and personal gifts.

Reinforce their worth every day by telling them that only God could make them so wonderful and full of wonder. A loving, encouraging voice comes to a child like a stream of music and strength. Let them know that they are special creations and that divine miracles are waiting to happen in their lives.

Children grow and change so quickly that we need to regularly attend to their spiritual awareness. Closely guide their lives; truly see your children and listen to what they say. Ask how they are feeling, and watch what they do. Be available to answer their questions with calm assurance that God is with them, watching over them and caring for them.

Children have so much to teach us that just their presence in our lives is a blessing from God. They are a reminder that we have so much to be grateful for.

Recognize children's worth and nurture their talents. The word "recognition" means "to know again," so let them know a gift comes from God, predetermined to help them help others. As they listen to their hearts, their hearts will tell them what that gift is.

Steer children to their strengths and guide their interests. Does she love drawing? Surprise her with enrollment in an art class. A budding writer? Take him to the library and attend story time. A swimming sensation? Try classes at the YMCA or a club. Maintain a positive viewpoint about their personal dreams and goals.

Of course there will be moments along the way when they may want to give up. That is the time for you to shine, encouraging children to have patience, to persist and succeed in the face of frustration. Eventually, they will achieve the goals they set for themselves with your wonderful guidance. A reader wrote, "My granddad used to take me to a small stream on our farm and he would point out to me a boulder or stone in the bed of the stream. Then, he would draw my attention to the many ripples upon the stream's surface and my granddad said, 'The stone or solitary boulder had no knowledge of the visible ripples it was causing upon the surface of somewhat harsh waters.' His comment has stayed with me through many dark days and challenging experiences."

You may feel alone and stuck in one place, but oh how you can affect the many young ones that pass by your way with your encouraging smiles and words. Friends and families need to provide encouragement and emotional support.

Make it a habit to say something appreciative about a child's every effort. Praise the small steps, for the life of every great man or woman started with small, insecure steps . . . but someone held out a warm, helping hand and spoke the revelation of confidence into their hearts.

You can be the giver of the gifts of self-confidence and the joyful expectation that leads to greatness. You can be the start of a great transformation in the lives of those around you.

You can be a miracle worker.

Exercise Lifts Your Spirit

One of the best gifts we can give ourselves is to nurture and take care of our bodies. When our bodies are in healthy harmony, we are more able to focus on our spiritual, mental, and emotional needs.

Let's respect our health and develop a daily maintenance program that will carry us joyfully into the years ahead. Lovingly care for this God-given temple.

You'll be amazed at what a big difference even the smallest adjustment in your diet and fitness routine can make.

A recent Duke University study found that loneliness and depression are the most common triggers of overeating in women. Exercise, which lifts the spirit as it burns the fat, can help to eliminate the blues. A brisk walk or a bike ride can do wonders. Strengthening exercises can build and tone your body and make you feel great. Use free weights to tone your muscles. Did you know that muscle uses more calories to maintain itself than other body tissue? So for every pound of muscle you put on, you automatically burn an extra forty to fifty calories a day.

Psychologists suggest turning to a friend instead of comfort foods and talking out your anxiety to make yourself feel better. Tackle problems without the help of food. Try not to eat when you are feeling stressed.

Sip a cup of herbal tea with honey, do some deep-breathing exercises, or take a warm bath to calm your nerves and help you feel more in control.

Have a good breakfast. It will help curb your appetite for the rest of the day and get your metabolism moving. Try getting up fifteen minutes earlier to enjoy a delicious breakfast. Pour apple juice over breakfast cereal instead of whole milk. For homemade muffins use applesauce in place of butter or oil in baking; replace butter on toast with jelly.

Healthful foods and snacks give you an energy lift, and should be kept within your reach. Keep a bowl of cool grapes or a container of cut raw vegetables in the refrigerator. Munch on fat-free whole-grain pretzels. A piece of fruit takes longer to consume and makes you feel fuller because it is loaded with fiber. Plus, it is lower in calories than fruit juice.

Experts recommend that you do at least thirty minutes of moderate aerobic activity three times a week for instant calorie burning, plus toning exercises to keep your metabolism primed.

Make meal times special. Arrange fresh flowers on the table and use pretty place mats and dishes. Listening to slow music during dinner can make you take smaller bites, chew longer, and eat slower. When you eat, don't watch television, read, or pay bills. Focus on having a great meal or talking with your family or friends. Savor each bite.

Clear the table as soon as you're finished to keep from sitting around and picking when you are no longer hungry. Ask your family to help you put away extra food after your meal, so you won't be tempted to pick at all the leftovers.

Remember the color rule. Fill your plate with colorful foods. The more colors on your plate, the more nutrients you are probably getting. Green beans, corn, tomatoes, carrots, beets. Get the picture?

For a chocolate craving, fat-free chocolate syrup can be your saving grace. Drizzle it on yogurt or fresh fruit for a delicious dessert, or try a nonfat chocolate sorbet.

Eat dinner early, between 5 and 6 P.M. Group studies concluded that among those who ate the same number of calories, those who ate earlier gained less weight and slept better.

Don't punish yourself if you have one bad eating day. Reflect on your accomplishments and reward yourself for your fitness victories. Experience the joy of each precious day. This will affirm that a fulfilling life does not focus on food.

Find the strength to overcome any obstacles that hinder your stamina. Increase your self-confidence, inner strength, and discipline by ending your day with a word of thanks to your loving Heavenly Father.

Do Not Waste the Precious Gift of Time

One of my favorite times of the day is the morning, when I can take a few priceless moments to sit still and reflect on the wonders of life.

There never seems to be enough of this precious, glorious, and fleeting gift. Time is a most-sought-after jewel—moments to spare, a minute to ponder, and time to absorb.

As my fingers press on the keyboard to write these words for you, I recall how precious every second is. Time is the only thing that never stops; it's always passing, so utilize it to the fullest.

Each day provides its own gifts; therefore, we must embrace the moment. Every day, each hour, this very instant, "busyness" is trying to keep our thoughts from looking upward and inward.

How are you using your time? What are you doing with this price-less gift? Always think of the phrase "carpe diem"—"seize the day"—and give yourself an opportunity to embrace the qualities of life that are unseen, such as love, peace, and joy.

We are so privileged to live in a land where we have the freedom to pursue whatever we want to gain in our lives. It's good to know that God is directing our footsteps and if we ask Him, He will gently lead us in the right direction.

There is a way to slow down and get more done. Sometimes we have to pretend the car won't start, the television set is broken, and the telephone disconnected. Every big business deal is going to be passed on to someone else someday. That also goes for your house, car, and your other possessions. There is no way to stop it, so make a portion of your day for yourself and your loved ones. Reassess your goals.

This is your life; spend your time wisely! Prioritize in importance what you need to focus your life around. Remember, you can't do everything, spend time with everyone, and go everywhere, so create a certain portion of each day to be formed into that priceless jewel of love, peace, and joy.

I find that I'm much happier if I do things that are in line with what God wants me to do. It is of utmost importance to me to be able to guide my children's thoughts to the beautiful handiwork of God and to know that when things happen that are sudden and hurtful, they can turn to Him for help.

While I was planting pansies out on our deck this summer, a bee stung me on my leg. I screamed to my husband for help, and when my two-and-a-half-year-old daughter saw that the bee stung her mommy, she cried. Later, when a friend of mine asked my daughter what Daddy did when Mommy got stung by the bee, she said, "Daddy prayed." I'm so happy to know that somehow I have been able to instill in her little mind the most important thing to do when emergencies arise. God sends us little reminders each day of His constant care. A valuable and fruitful life can be found by keeping in touch with God each day.

Though the trees grow taller and their branches wider, time doesn't seem to affect them. They reach up their arms to God, and they are our constant reminders to praise Him.

May this be the start of a time of new beginnings, filled with God's blessings. Reflect on all that He has done for you and on all that He has promised to do. God is nothing but love, understanding, and forgiveness. Sure, we find ourselves in circumstances that we have reaped from what we have sown in the past, but now we can make time to start sowing some beautiful seeds of indescribable sweetness as we ask God to open our eyes and our hearts to His love.

Remember the Many Gifts Given to You

God loves each one of us as though we were the only one He had to love. Count on and trust in His love. There's nothing like it. We are the jewels in His crown. Be aware of the many facets and depths of rich beauty within you.

The joys and treasures to be discovered are unlimited, as many as there are stars in the heavens. God has made us to be rich in character. Treasures such as genuine friendships, deep love, and a personal relationship with God are flashes of glorious color from within the jewel that you are.

Celebrate your self-worth every day, not just on a holiday, birthday, or anniversary. Appreciate the wonderful individual that you are becoming. Grow into a greater awareness of God's attributes within you; learn to give more of yourself to laugh fully and deeply with joy. You will grow more beautiful with each passing day.

Don't forget to tend to your own special needs, wants, and aspirations. Freeing yourself should be a priority. Even an hour of walking in nature will work wonders on your spirit and soul. Buy yourself a rose, study it, and drink in its velvety beauty and heady scent. Play your favorite music and be the conductor, or snuggle in a wingback chair and become what you read.

Nurturing and doing special things for your own enjoyment is very important. If you absorb life to its fullest, you will have much more life to give.

Life can sometimes be like a garden that has been neglected for a while. There are weeds and also exquisite flowers. You can take whatever you choose and make a bouquet of your own. If you rush and scurry about, hurrying to procure, you may end up with more weeds than flowers.

It's such a beautiful, creative time to live—don't take any part of it for granted. Every moment is sacred, every moment is blessed, and every moment is one that we may not have had except for the grace of God.

The wise person goes slowly, searches, and finds the rarest bloom. Even if it is in the middle of a thorn bed, they will reach it. Let nothing stop you from the best. You, too, can have that exquisite flower. Surely, you will receive the prize.

The only attitude to have is true thankfulness and appreciation for all the wonderful gifts of life and love that God has put within you. Find a friend who shares the realization of this outlook and appreciates the gifts within, someone you can communicate with and receive love from. When two people together are in agreement, they inspire each other and build each other up. Develop those special relationships with others— those who are your true family, the children of God.

Make a list today of twenty great things about you. Remember the good things others have said. Forget the negative; it's not important. Some of the most important things in life are to have a giving heart, share encouragement, smooth out problems, and enjoy a wonderful sense of humor. If you have these qualities, you can get through anything.

When you realize who you are, you are much more powerful and are thoroughly successful. When you are using the gifts that God gave you, I believe you have a greater sense of your full potential and can achieve greater heights of creativity than you ever dreamed.

Let me start your list. Write at the top that you are thoughtful and caring, or you wouldn't have read this essay to the end. What wonderful attributes . . . I am so thankful for you!

Fill Each Day with Joy and Trust

One day at a time, lived well and strung together, makes a beautiful garland of life.

It is a challenge in itself to live each day to the fullest. This doesn't necessarily mean being busy at something all the time. Life is living and just relishing every minute, while meditating on the fact that God is aware, this very moment, of you. On this fact alone, as children of God, we should be rejoicing every day. He cares for you and has given you the instruction book of life, the Bible. Read it and do the very best that you can with every day that you are given. Fill your mind and heart with thoughts of peace, joy, hope, and victory.

"You changed my day," a friend said as I offered advice about a situation that was troubling her. "I feel so much better," she exclaimed. "Your faith is contagious."

Many obstacles stall our momentum to success by paralyzing us with perplexity. Concentrate solely on each day's work by shutting out all other thoughts and hindrances.

Take every thought that concerns you to the Lord. His wisdom is beyond all we can imagine. He will take care of you and provide for all your needs. I recall that the Bible says, "My grace is sufficient for you. My strength is made perfect in your weakness."

By worrying about the future, we stunt our progress. Stressing about what might happen or feeling anxiety over a situation that we have no control over robs us of this most precious day. Limit your worries by doing what you can for the moment and putting it in God's hands. Sir William Osler, a Canadian physician, said, "Draw a circle around one twenty-four-hour period of time and don't bother your mind with worries about what you need to accomplish outside of that."

By habit, we may be tense about tomorrow, next week, or next month, but pull victories from times in the past when God has given you grace. See how God changes things and works things together for good.

This is where a bedside journal is really helpful. Just jotting down the date and time that God has provided, solved, and changed the gloom to glory in the past will be an encouragement to you all your life, to your children and their children thereafter. So start one now, a note or two of thanks to God for what He has done for you each day. That is what a friend of mine has done for many years, and she says her life has been a "journey of miracles." You might only add to your journal once a month, but months turn into years, years of miraculous intervention.

You're honoring God by not fretting and trusting instead. By doing this you'll find the nervousness, which is human, goes away.

As life swirls around us with concerns for our children, deadlines to meet, and endless chores to do, we find ourselves overwhelmed. But when we concentrate on the minutes in our lives that we give to family devotion and receiving God's unchanging love, we walk with sure and steady steps.

Life's great moments are in the pure contentment of small pleasures enjoyed now to the fullest. Think on the past, in quiet contemplation of its victories.

When I consider how God has intervened for me, when I couldn't see a solution anywhere, I grow joyful and strong in faith because I know, as I trust in Him, He will do it for me again and again and again. And as you trust in Him, dear readers, He will do it for you . . . again and again and again.

Let the World Know You by Your Smile

In the morning, before I leave for work, I put all my cares into God's hands. By the time I finish talking to Him, I've stopped my frowning and a sweet smile of peace and trust has dawned upon my face.

Numerous studies have shown that when you smile, pressure is put upon strategic nerve points in your face that contribute to the release of endorphins, which create a sense of well-being. So, today, immerse yourself in your own wonderful smile and notice other people's smiles. Give one out in exchange for one back, from faces of little children, teenagers, young adults, and the elderly. Tuck them into your heart until it's bursting with joy.

A smile costs nothing but its value is priceless, so begin now to share one with those that you meet, giving a pleasant response, a kind word, and good cheer to show evidence of love for your fellow human beings. A smile is remembered more than a name. How many times have you thought, "I remember their face but not their name?"

Do you know that your smile can even carry through the telephone lines? A smile conveys happiness, joy, and love. It says, "I like you," "I'm happy to see you." Soon, others will react with the same kindness that you show.

Smiling changes your whole outlook on life and can change the mood of people who see you smile. A smile is like a yawn . . . it's catching!

Keep your face to the sunny side of the street and you'll never walk in the shadow. There are so many things to smile and be happy about. It's easy to see the joy in each precious day if you refuse to acknowledge any passing shower. There will always be a cloud somewhere, so here are ways to fly above them.

- Find a moment or two in your busy schedule to stop and watch little children at play. It wasn't that long ago that you were young and played dress-up or made go-carts out of wooden crates. You can smile back at each child with the child within yourself.
- Read a funny cartoon in the newspaper or in a magazine for a good chuckle. When one reminds you of a friend's situation, cut it out, stuff it in an envelope signed with love, and send it off to them.
- For great fun, collect those grandchildren or the kids on the block and have a "clown party." Make costumes with lots of funny old hats, big clothes, and face painting, or buy fake glasses with the nose and mustache attached. Have prizes for the funniest joke and the best clown face and create memories never to be forgotten. Tell each child the importance of seeing the humorous side of life, for this will balance out the sad things they all must encounter.
- Make a scrapbook. Ask one of the children in your life to go through a stack of old magazines, photographs, and newspaper clippings to make a "happy scrapbook" full of pictures of tail-wagging pets, joyous mementos, and funny cartoons. Keep the scrapbook handy, and whenever they come to visit again, you can reminisce as you look back on all the happy times.
- "Smile at each other, smile at your wife, smile at your husband, smile at your children, smile at each other—it doesn't matter who it is—and that will help you grow up in greater love," said Mother Teresa. A friend of mine often looks up and just smiles at God.

I know the Bible says in Psalm 98, "Make a joyful noise before the Lord." God created you to be happy, and happiness creates the permanent expression of smiling eyes. Smiles of joy, smiles of understanding, and smiles of love. Your smile is a beauty beyond measure to give to the world.

Take Special Care of the Body God Gave You

Your body is a grand temple, a magnificent creation, all parts working together in unity to help you enjoy every moment of this God-given life. Take care of yourself with intelligence and respect.

The care you give your body is one of the most important responsibilities you will ever have. How you perceive your needs directs your actions, thoughts, and achievements. So choose to cherish and honor this sacred dwelling. Provided by God our Father, it is the vehicle He gave us to take us joyfully through this journey called life.

The Lord loves an even balance, so to stay healthy emotionally, spiritually, and physically, we need to have control over our vocation, recreation, and restoration.

Endorse healthy habits. Nourish your body with wholesome foods and pure, clean water. Engage in a regular fitness routine. Take a brisk walk in the sunlight. Walking is one of the best forms of exercise there is. "It takes a direct dispensation from Heaven to become a walker," wrote Henry David Thoreau. Walk for your spirit and soul, as well as for your physical well-being.

Stay up-to-date on your medical exams, checkups, and dental care. Don't smoke, and stay away from alcohol. Take vitamins. Many people need vitamin supplements to feel their best.

Spend time alone. Quiet moments in solitude can create times of personal reflection and give restoration to body and soul. Carve leisure time out of your busy schedule for your own enjoyment. Discuss with your spouse the importance of sharing your thoughts, being your own person, and having time alone. You'll be surprised how much more patience you'll have with others after a few hours of peace and solitude.

Do what makes you personally happy. Try a new sport, plan an exciting vacation, or delve into a hobby. Go to the gym or to tag sales with friends. Take dancing lessons with your mate, or browse through a bookstore for an interesting novel.

Be intellectually stimulated. Continually try to reach higher heights of thought. Communicate with a trusted confidant, and talk out your dreams and aspirations.

Give yourself a break. Find ways to renew and recharge. Indulge in a "day of beauty" at a local salon. You deserve it! Unwind with a soothing facial, a manicure, pedicure, or an herbal shampoo. Pamper yourself and feel rejuvenated. Take deep breaths and breathe out any stress and negativity.

Look your best. Confidence will radiate from the inside out when you feel you look great. A sparkle in your eye and humorous thoughts in your mind will convey joie de vivre. Watch your posture. Buy that pretty scarf or new tie. Dress up for dinner and put candles on the table and listen to classical music. Don't hold back in creating an atmosphere of pure delight.

Keep spiritually centered. Put God first in your life and thank Him for your blessings. Begin each day in gratitude and express to God your plans for the future.

Join a prayer group, read passages from the Bible, or sing spiritual songs to brighten your hours. He will send showers of blessings upon you.

Smile and be happy. Enjoy the wonderful world God has made for us. "Thou hast created all things and for thy pleasure they are created."—Revelation 4:11.

You can't be so heavenly minded that you are no earthly good . . . So let's take extra-special care of this God-given temple. Ask the Lord to help you achieve an even balance and peace in both mind and body.

All things work together for the good when you respect the one and only body God has given to you. Remember, it's the house of your beautiful soul.

Dig Out the Root of Bitterness and Love Thrives

The sweetest victories in life come from overcoming hard circumstances.

Life is a testing ground. Great beauty is revealed in wisely enduring the trials we go through. That supernatural internal beauty is the character of patience, kindness, and persistence.

To live this life victoriously and successfully, we must continually keep the root of bitterness out of our hearts. We all have trials. We must decide whether they will cause us to become embittered old men and women or whether we will conquer the root of bitterness with forgiving love.

Some people have let bitterness grow so deep, they are unable to trust, believe, or hope again. But the Word of God is true and I know it says that God never gives us more than we can bear. So no matter the test, we must trust and never doubt Him. I remember that the Word also says to cast your cares upon Him. That's truly the only way you can bear all things.

You've heard the saying, "Nip it in the bud." If we don't stop the bitterness that wells up within us because of the single action of one individual, it becomes like crabgrass. It grows and grows—it invades and spoils everything in your life. I read in the Bible, "The devil walks about like a roaring lion seeking who he can devour." But the rest of the verse says, "Greater is He that is within us than he that is within the world." Look what happens when we give up and get rid of the bitterness . . . we outsmart the enemy. Let's realize that the trial was only one small incident in our whole life. When we keep it contained to that one small circumstance and pray about it, God will give us the grace to show His love to the person who wronged us. Then we have become mighty conquerors.

Do not continue to discuss a negative situation or mention it again. The more you talk about it, the more it stays alive. If someone does something to offend you, return that evil with good.

Connect with God through prayer. Share your thoughts openly and comfortably with Him. Get so close to God that nothing will offend you. Don't be full of resentment. It will hurt you more than it hurts the other person. Let it go and drop it in the sea of forgetfulness. Pray and show overcoming love, for it's written, "Love never fails."

Leave all bitterness, malice, and strife behind and rejoice over the wonderful things in your life. There are so many. Be like the lovely trees, arms up and outstretched, thanking God for every beautiful thing we have.

This great revelation will give you freedom and renew your youth like the eagle. God is in control. Never be upset with Him for what He allows. He has a reason for all that He does, and it is to bring out the finest in you. There is reassurance always to be found in our Heavenly Father's care.

Dig out the roots of bitterness. Lay the ax to the root of that tree. Let the handle of that ax read, "Faith in God" and "Restore unto me the joy of the Lord." Swing it and sever that root. When that life-sapping tree falls, in its place rise the rose of Sharon and lovely lily of the valley.

And up above it, in the soft dawn of the sky, the bright morning star shines upon the beauty of your soul.

Let Your Home Express All the Beauty of Life

A beautiful home creates the backdrop for living a beautiful life. It's a place where memories are made. Re-dream, remodel, reflect, rearrange, and rev up your home.

You are the one who makes it happen, so begin the transformation today. Let the love that shines from your eyes be reflected in your home.

Make a house a warm, welcoming, and lovely place by surrounding yourself with rainbow colors. Create an inviting dwelling in which to raise a family, entertain friends, live, and relax. Find comfort, tranquility, and well-being as you decorate.

Express yourself by adding your own personal signature. Your experiences and your delightful personality will shine through every room as you add your personal touch.

Your environment tells who you are, so create your own unique background through a romantic style, a country setting, French provincial, or modern simplicity. Whether it's one room or a castle, make your home come alive with your special touch.

- Make a long hallway or stairwell become your art gallery or photo gallery. Let the faces of those you love smile on you every day.
- Bring color home by the rainbow-full. Periwinkle blue is a cool and calming color, perfect for a restful touch in the bedroom. Yellow is a bit of sunshine and an energetic color for any living room. Green is nature's hue, so cozy and relaxing. Some decorating experts say that every room needs a small touch of black to add sophistication. So add a piece of wrought iron or a beautiful black marble pedestal.

- Flowers make the home come alive. Permanent silk arrangements require little maintenance. The scent of fresh-cut flowers such as gardenias or simple honeysuckle makes the home smell heavenly.
- Beautiful music can create the perfect backdrop for soothing reading or conversation. Turn off the television and put on your favorite music. It can transform your whole attitude.
- Accent a child's room by using custom borders. For example, design a gazebo headboard and accent it with borders and flowering vines. Add dolly-and-teddy-bear-attended tea tables and chairs of wicker. Use glow-in-the-dark borders and ceiling stars to create a night of wonder for a small boy to fall asleep in.
- For a peaceful and tranquil baby's room, do what we did. Sponge-paint fluffy white clouds onto blue walls, encircling the whole room with a border of angels amid the same fluffy clouds. Accessorize with angel accents and a lovely white canopy veiling cascading from the ceiling over the crib.
- Bring the outdoors in with tall ficus trees and ferns, adding tiny white lights for evening glamour.
- Use storage boxes tucked in closets or under bed skirts to combat clutter. Pretty hatboxes can contain sewing paraphernalia.
- If there are small children in the house, select fabrics with bright patterns and colors to help disguise inevitable accidents. Upholster furniture in dark velvets and deep damasks for winter, and then switch to slipcovers in white or flowered chintz for a total summer change.

Remember the five God-given senses as you decorate and create: sight, touch, taste, smell, and sound. Also remember that no home is of any value without love. Even if you cannot afford to do anything else, you can afford to decorate your home in the golden glow of love. And as Goethe said, "He is the happiest, be he king or peasant, who finds peace in his home."

Daily Exercise Will Benefit the Body

Look great and feel wonderful! Give your body a tune-up. Put the oil of peace in your mind and the spark of joy in your soul.

A few simple changes in your physical fitness care can give you more confidence in both mind and body. Increasing energy with the fuel of daily inspiration and exercise can eliminate many health problems and may overall make you a more positive and optimistic person.

Exercise can restore a sense of well-being and a more youthful nature. A commitment to working out regularly is one of the best things you can do for yourself and for your family. So include your children, parents, friends, or loved ones in enjoying physical fitness as a part of the normal routine of your life. Here are a wealth of ideas to partake in. (As always, consult with your doctor before beginning any new workout routine.)

Variety is the key to a boredom-free workout. Keep in shape and start moving! Take one step at a time . . . the momentum will take over from there. Look at your schedule to see how you can incorporate your exercise habit into your day. Treat your exercise routine like an appointment. Write it on your calendar so you have a designated time. Plan your workout and stick to it. Soon, it will happily become a way of life.

Walking is one of the best overall exercises for everyone. Walk at lunchtime with a coworker to brainstorm ideas, or take your pet for a walk.

A walk in the park, biking in the countryside, or a jog along the shoreline can give you variety, as well as a change of scenery. Start slowly; forget the "no pain, no gain" approach. Develop a consistent game plan that starts out conservatively.

The American College of Sports Medicine recommends thirty minutes of cardiovascular exercise three times a week and also strength training at least twice a week. Warm up five to ten minutes before your workout to raise your body temperature and to stretch your muscles. Be sure to cool down after exercising as well.

Do leg lifts while talking on the phone, sit-ups when you are listening to a book on tape, or ride a stationary bike while reading. I bought a treadmill and exercise early in the morning, before the children wake up.

Seek support from others. Turn to your spouse or a close friend for encouragement to get you through every plateau. Try exercising with a partner. Positive praise and words like "you're doing great" and "keep with it" can help you stay on track. Being there for your workout partner is added incentive to help you stay with your program.

Buy your children equipment or toys that promote physical activity. Select fitness-oriented gifts with the recipient's skills and interests in mind.

Have a family fitness day. Take turns letting each child pick an activity to do that day. It could be swimming, canoeing, horseback riding, or roller-skating. At a picnic, organize a badminton or volleyball game.

Exercise to music. Research shows that music lowers your perception of fatigue. You'll be more likely to keep going if you like the tunes.

Run errands on foot. Walk to the grocery store if you just need a few items. Return library books or walk to the office if you live close by. You'll forget you're exercising because you'll be having such a good time.

Exercise to feel good; looking great is just a fringe benefit. This action plan can help you get a head start. Set your goals and make the emphasis the importance of good health and a joy-filled life. Your mind and body will thank you.

We Thrive on Lots and Lots of Loving Hugs!

Know the bumper sticker that reads, "Have you hugged your child today?"

Well, this phrase needs to be posted everywhere. Research shows that touch is a powerful communicator that can improve well-being and self-esteem.

Child development experts agree that the single most important element for a child's happy life is loving physical contact. Being raised with an abundance of pats on the back, hugs, and kisses goes further toward producing happy adults than being raised with any other advantage.

Another study also suggests that children who are hugged a lot find more satisfaction in all areas of their adult life, including friendships, careers, and marriage.

Your arms were made with the number-one purpose of hugging the children in your life. They watch you closely and learn from you. Be a positive role model to the children. Use polite words yourself, especially when you are addressing a child. Your child will learn kind manners from your example.

Loving words are an endearing demonstration of care and respect. Words such as "please," "thank you," and "excuse me" show a good upbringing. Say "I love you" often. This will reinforce security and contentment.

We all want to feel as though we are here for a special reason. American philosopher William James wrote, "The deepest principle of human nature is the craving to be appreciated and the desire to be important." Treat everyone you meet as if they had an invisible sign on their heart that says, "I need to know you appreciate me." Then, respond to that sign immediately. People will react positively to you if they are made to feel important, respected, and needed.

Hold hands with a child, take a nature walk, and teach them to hug a tree and kiss a flower. Hunker down with him or her and study a caterpillar. Explain how it will become a lovely butterfly one day. Advise children that they, too, will change, grow, and become even more beautiful.

Have family mealtime. A routine such as having dinner together creates a sense of predictability and security for all family members. Say a prayer of thanksgiving and share happy thoughts. Play with your children. Have a tea party with your daughter, play hide-and-seek, or make a picture on the driveway with chalk. Give kids your undivided, uninterrupted time and all of your attention when they talk to you. They will gain confidence from your full focus. This is like saying, "I really care about you."

Share a family group hug, and include the dog! Take time to do things together.

Tell your children that they are special. Cuddle together with a book each day. Put your arm around the child or sit a toddler on your lap. Reading to a child builds language skills and imparts a fondness for the written word.

Actions do speak louder than words, so be patient, cheery, and helpful. When problems arise, be optimistic and let kids know that they will grow wiser every day as time goes on. If you are feeling down, show your child how to dispel the gloominess and communicate positive things you can do that make you feel better. Try listening to your favorite music, doing a craft project, collecting seashells at the shore, talking to a loved one, or helping someone in need.

Show children the stars at night and teach them how to pray. Listening to their prayers is a wonderful experience, for out of the mouths of babes come gems. You will be able to carry a whole treasure chest back to your bed, and when we add our own precious words of thanks, it's our way of giving God a hug!

Live This Day; Stop Dwelling on the Past

*I*t has been said that most people spend their life worrying about things . . . and 90 percent of those things never happen.

The plague of worry is something that we all do. Today, we will try to eliminate this habit. Worrying is a thief, and it robs you of life—past, present, and future.

Each day is a new beginning. Put the past behind you and enjoy every moment of the joy and happiness that only this day can bring. Let nothing disturb your peace of mind. Know that if you continually worry about a situation, you stifle the creative ability to solve the problem.

If you take a positive outlook and expect the best, the problem can reverse itself and become a blessing. A sense of humor can actually dispel the paralyzing effect of worry. Try to see the humorous side to a situation.

"A good belly laugh can heighten relaxation and build a stronger immune system," suggests a study by the Humor Project, an organization in New York, which studies the effects of humor on the body.

Adopt a childlike perspective. Whenever you begin to worry about a circumstance, ask yourself, "How would a seven-year-old see this situation?" By reframing worry through a child's eyes, you can't help but laugh and thus relieve distress.

Do not manufacture problems in your mind. Situations should be seen for what they are, not inflated by fearful or negative thoughts. Empty your mind continually of regrets, resentment, or bad feelings.

What would happen if you drove your car by looking in the rearview mirror? You would hit something. That's what happens when you worry and dwell on the past. Just think of the best possible outcome and it will prevent unhealthy thoughts from clouding your perception of the future. Think of a problem this way: "Will this situation matter ten years from now?"

If something is bothering you, sit down and make a list of your feelings. Sometimes seeing the issue on paper and writing down a solution cannot only simplify your cares, but can also bring an answer. Share your troubles or concerns with a trusted friend. It helps so much to have someone to confide in, talk with, or get advice from. Having someone as a sounding board can make it seem less menacing.

Lift up your worries to God. He is in control and will reveal to you that all this focus on material gain, or worrying about what other people think, or about physical imperfections is just stealing the joy of living.

Affirm and confirm His help, grace, and guidance even before they are given. God's promises are glorious. Let nothing disturb you. Let nothing frighten you, for God is with you and will see you through. Hand over the problem to His care. He will work it out according to His wisdom and purpose. Remember this: God never gives grace for your imagination, but He gives abundant grace for reality.

We are little creators; we set the atmosphere in our homes. So begin today to dispel worry and replace it with faith.

Have you ever heard the story about the man who took his problems to the Lord in prayer and put them on His altar? He came back in only five minutes, took them down again, and worried over them. Then he put them back on the altar. He repeated this same scenario for thirty days. Finally, he asked God, "Why haven't you taken care of all my worries?" God replied, "If you would have just left them totally with me . . . they would have been solved in three days."

Can you take better care of your worries than God can? Having done all you can, just leave the problems with Him and walk away. "In God have I put my trust: I will not be afraid." —Psalm 56:11.

Begin to live again and enjoy life; we have only one. Let's live it happily and full of faith.

Take Time to Appreciate Quiet Moments

*T*he rush, hustle, and bustle of life seems so frantic lately, it feels good just to sit here quietly in isolation and do nothing. Though my mind races at a record high speed, as I'm sure yours does, on the twenty-plus things I must get done before tomorrow, I find it suddenly very important to take time out for soothing moments of sacred quietness.

Life can become so intense, we feel there are just not enough hours in a day, juggling families, careers, chores, etc. This inner stress can make you ill. So give yourself permission to enjoy the peace and tranquility of seclusion, moments of renewal.

There is an enemy who wants to speed things up and put a whole bunch of problems in our path, like the waving arms of a basketball guard, so we feel overwhelmed, confused, and don't know which way to turn. But we have a choice to stop for a second, turn around from all that stress and negativity, and make our goal.

Take a minute now to slow down, take a deep breath, and savor life more completely. Take this opportunity to heal the body and quiet the soul, to bring balance and harmony into your heart once again. Taking time out is the best cure for stress.

Think of quiet intervals in the day as a long-term investment in your peace of mind and quality of life. If you are experiencing anxiety, take a break from whatever is causing you the pressure. It's okay to do nothing, to spend an afternoon alone.

Life moves so quickly, if you don't stop and look around once in a while, you could miss it. Bring a tea tray outdoors, a bowl of fresh fruit, and an inviting book to help you regroup. Be calm and still. Sit back passively and observe the restorative beauty of creation.

Behold the majesty of the glorious world that God created for our pleasure. Nature is like a form of medication that acts as a healing balm over your entire being.

Take solitude in the morning, before the beginning of the day; or perhaps it would be more convenient in the evening, after the children have gone to sleep. Schedule your quiet time and adhere to it.

In quietness and confidence you possess your soul. In silence you can collect your thoughts and ideas. Even presidents take a day or weekend to be at peace and think.

We become too much creatures of time. To God there is no time. So let's walk with Him for a little bit each day. His peace surpasses all the substitutes the world has to offer. Being alone can give your creative spirit a chance to recoup. Idleness is not always uncreative.

What can be more idle than sleep? But God has made us so we must take in a certain amount of hours to sleep and be still, so we will be refreshed and restored for the day that lies ahead.

When we are asleep, we are unconscious of that restoration, but He also made us so we could take moments of quietness when we are awake and be wise enough to take in His thoughts and restore our minds to right thinking.

Nighttime is beginning to fall and the misty earth is starting to turn a pearl gray. The sky is brushed with amethyst and the setting sun edges the clouds with pure gold. As dusk nears, the sound of cooing doves and the sweet chirps of the birds, last lingering bits of praise, soothe our souls.

It feels as though God is so near. How lovingly, gently, and peacefully He lulls the world to sleep. Like a mother pulling a down comforter over her newborn baby, so the Lord pulls a blanket of night clouds over us. This evening will give us a chance to rest, to be refreshed and rejuvenated for the glorious day that awaits us tomorrow.

Release Anger and Restore Peace

I like to remember that God said, "I am the light of the world. Who so ever believes in me shall never walk in darkness." Turn on the light in your life. Let the radiance of God come into a dark mind and give a soft, peaceful glow. Light and darkness cannot dwell together in the same room, so lift His Word up high above everything else. Honor it first and you will see clearly. Leave your heart open with a willingness to consider Him, and allow God to transform you by His brilliant light.

Light is revelation, understanding, and wisdom. Treat yourself to His beautiful Word and bask in the presence of the Lord's love.

Forget the past and let this radiant beam shine on the future. Opportunities abound. You cannot go back in time and begin again, but you can start today to make a new and exciting tomorrow.

Your life is full of a great and vast array of possibilities. We each have a host of angels around us to spur us onward and upward. There are more with us who walk in God's Word than all the negative forces against us.

Within your heart, turn on the light of love and forgiveness for those who have wronged you. This will make the enemy powerless. The power of God's love is stronger than anything. Your determination and perseverance may not immediately change them, but it will completely transform you for the better.

Illuminate your life by practicing forgiveness. When you love and completely forgive, you have a strength that makes it impossible for anything or any person to hurt you. Try saying before bedtime: "I forgive and love this person who has done me wrong because you, God, have forgiven me." Upon wakening, your spirit will be enlightened and your mind and body changed from one burdened with stress to one that is wonderfully content and peaceful. This simple practice will work wonders.

God's wisdom eliminates anger, hatred, and resentment. Do not waste your precious days on these negative emotions. They can harm you very much and can injure others, even those that you don't want to hurt. Don't be preoccupied with other people's sins. This only leaves you open to oppression and depression. Pray for them once and put them in God's hands and leave them there.

Just continue rejoicing in the Lord and focusing on all the blessings in your life.

Even when times are dark, we can sweeten the bitter by considering the deep compassion of God. Through adversity, we can emerge stronger, wiser, and more resilient. This is His will for us. Light a candle of hope with a prayer of faith, and a believing patience will bring forth the answer. Rely on God's strength in trying times. He is with you and has a purpose for what He allows. He will protect us and keep us.

Use your talents to shape the world for the better. Every caring act has a rippling effect touching many lives. Talk with each other about the goodness of the Lord. It is a profitable practice that will fill your heart with joy and lift you out of this dimension to God's presence. We have the power to influence others and to do so much good. Positive faith can bring light to your neighbors; it can heal and work miracles.

You, as believers, are part of this light of the world. You can make a difference. I know the Bible says, "Let your light shine before others so that they may see your good works and glorify your Father which is in Heaven." Rejoicing in the Lord creates a beam of light in the spiritual atmosphere. And the angels know it's the glory of God and flock around you. How joyful He makes our lives, full of hope, comfort, and peace which surpasses all understanding.

With a soft curtain of light, God's love is like the golden glow of the aurora borealis, wrapping around and enveloping your soul.

Eat Well and Lose Weight

*E*ating is meant to be one of life's grand pleasures. Preparing a meal, setting a beautiful table, and enjoying the company of good friends can be a wonderful experience.

In order to live, our bodies need food, the source of fuel needed to be converted into energy. But for many, food is their enemy, shortening lives and making them prone to indigestion, obesity, and heart attacks.

Respect the healthy laws of nature and fulfill that need to indulge by eating food that is both nutritious and appealing. Break the yo-yo dieting syndrome and let us use a commonsense approach to weight loss. Get your body in harmony with regular exercise, nourish your soul with prayer and meditation, eat wholesome food when you're hungry, and drink pure water when you thirst. Thank the Lord that we have these choices within our reach . . . for many do not.

Self-respect will help you possess a positive body image, and pounds will melt away. That is one of the only weight-loss tools you'll ever need.

Regular exercise is one of the most important things you can do for yourself. Exercise will strengthen the heart muscle. It's life enhancing. Keep your body moving! Thirty minutes of aerobic activities at least three times a week can restore energy to a listless life. (Be sure to check with your doctor before beginning any diet or fitness program.)

- Eat breakfast like a king, lunch like a queen, and dinner like a pauper.
- Before reaching for a snack, take one minute to focus on why you're eating. Are you physically hungry, or are you just bored or anxious? Try jogging around the block to help you relax. Then, reach for a piece of fruit or raw vegetables with a fat-free dip.
- Begin your meal with a bowl of broth-based soup. Soup has the

ability to quell hunger and is psychologically satisfying.

- Learn portion control. Appropriate meat portions should be the size of a deck of cards; a helping of rice or pasta should be the size of your fist.
- When going out to dinner with your spouse or a close friend, order one entree and two salads. Split the entree and save half of the calories. Plus, it is fun to share. Choose lean meats, fish, or poultry, and plenty of vegetables.
- Drink plenty of water. It helps your body expel toxic chemicals and metabolizes fat. Water is the secret to good health, glowing skin, and weight loss. We often mistake thirst for hunger, so drink eight to ten glass of water a day to help stave off food urges.
- Schedule classes, gardening, and other distracting activities for the times when the cookie jar calls out.
- Use positive images. Visualize how you will look and feel once you begin that exercise program or have lost those five pounds.
- Reduce temptations. Try brushing your teeth after eating to avoid picking and snacking.
- Limit your sodium intake. Check food labels and avoid salty foods. Use lemon juice, herbs, and spices in place of salt in recipes.
- Consume lots of dark green leafy vegetables like spinach, which has few calories and lots of calcium. Increase your fiber intake by eating whole fruits and veggies rather than drinking their juices.

It helps to have a caring person to share in your frustration of slow weight loss and to rejoice with you when the ten, twenty, thirty, or more pounds come off. So, dear readers, I am here with you and for you, to glory in your success and encourage you through your setbacks. I'll be using these tips, too, so together we can live a full, healthy, happy, and balanced life.

Don't Let Another Precious Moment Pass You By

*W*hat if God said, "Whatever they choose to read or watch will remain within them and will become a part of them and never leave their minds, but will be revealed in their actions from this day forward?" Wouldn't we really guard our hearts and be careful about what we watch, listen to, or participate in?

God has desired our lives to be lived beautifully in all He has given us. But in our pursuits of material wealth, in the hustle and bustle of life, and by spending all that time watching television and videos, we sometimes lose track of what's really important. Time goes by so quickly, so it's up to you to be the navigator and set your compass on God, who is in the realm of the North Star and never changes. He has given us the instruction book of life—the Bible—and if we choose to set our sights on the right course, we will reach our destination and not be shipwrecked.

Every morning, when we greet the day, let us open our eyes, take that first breath, and realize that this day is a special gift from God—a day to rejoice and be glad in.

Direct your thoughts to God. Nothing can dim the light that shines from within when the glory of the Lord is revealed. Neither heights nor depths, nor principalities nor powers can separate us from the love of God. With joyful expectation, read His Word and ask for the revelation of it to live by.

During the day, if opportunity affords, take your lunch to a park and ponder on a peaceful scene, admiring the beauty of nature, for it reveals God's lovely character. Then, praise and thank Him for all of His beautiful creation.

Spend more time with your precious family; they are God's gifts to you. Loving them is what brings a loving atmosphere into your home. Remember the quote, "The family that prays together stays together." That is the foundation for a solid, close, strong, and lasting family. Tell your spouse, children, and even your pets how much you love them. Give them a hug and do it now or as soon as you see them.

Give love freely. What you give out will come back, so sow love. Your attitude will mold your environment; begin changing it now because God loves a cheerful giver.

Appreciate your blessings and thank God liberally. Gratitude works miracles and adjusts your thinking. Remember, the most important mindset is the "attitude of gratitude." Invite friends as well as strangers you meet at church or work to your home. Don't wait until "someday" for these things. Bake a scrumptious dessert and invite a neighbor over to enjoy a cup of tea or coffee and really get to know each other.

Apologize for past squabbles. Never let a little dispute ruin a great friendship. Mend fences and plant flowers of love and trust beneath them.

Don't put off till tomorrow what you can do today. Start each day with prayer and ask God to open the way to letting His perfect will be done in your life. Read the Word, become the Word, watch the beauty of God's nature, and become more beautiful.

Test these things . . . and see how your quality of life improves.

The best days of our lives are right now! Let us savor them, so when we reminisce years from now, we can see for ourselves that God has transformed us . . . with His love.

Determine Now Your Own Character

S hakespeare wrote, "This above all: to thine own self be true, and it must follow, as the night the day, thou canst not then be false to any man."

Always be yourself. Always be the same. True beauty is in your own character, when you become the person God made you to be from the foundations of the world.

Each one of us has our own unique character made up of dreams, aspirations, and talents. These gifts were put within you so that you could bless the world with your special touch. Take the gift of encouragement and give it freely. When one hand reaches to another and another, soon we are all lifted one step higher. "Blessed are they which hunger and thirst after righteousness: for they shall be filled."—Matthew 5:6.

Your life can be the joy you want it to be, but you must strive to be sincerely yourself.

Ask God to lead you, and His grace will keep you as you venture out. We have to continually remember that we all make mistakes and fall. For sincere mistakes, God gives mercy and forgiveness. It is not how many times you fall that counts; it's how many times you get up. So get up and light your candle again. Shine it at home, shine it at work, shine it at school—let it shine.

You have been given a corner of this earth to enrich and enlighten. You are one of a kind. God made you to be a reflection of His great diversity, like the variety of flowers.

What would happen if we awoke one morning and all the roses had daisy petals stuck onto the tips of their petals or if all the sparrows had peacock feathers in their wings? They would certainly not be able to fly.

And so this is what happens when we strive to be someone else instead of ourselves. It is the beginning of something ridiculous, and our spirits, which were meant to soar, never get off the ground. God has made you to be beautiful, noble, and true. As the lovely moon in the heavens reflects the sun, we must be reflecting the glory of the Son. Second Corinthians 3:18 says, "We all, with open hearts must look at Him as if we were looking in a mirror, then we will be changed from glory to glory."

There is a treasure hidden deep within your heart. What a wonderful discovery this can be. Everyone in their right mind wants to do kind things for others. And the happiness it brings is doubled when they express their thanks. Some may not show their thankfulness. This is where God's love must take over human love and continue our goodness to that person. Some might be embittered and hardened over past hurts. But just a little of God's love applied daily never fails.

As the rain refreshes the wilting flower, let the joy of being the real you bring back the joy of life to them. Read God's Word and gain the wisdom that overcomes, the peace that passes all understanding, and the love that never fails.

For as these seeds fall into your soul, you will find that they begin to bloom and become the precious rainbow colors that radiate from your inner being, and it will become so easy to be yourself.

You have been created by the One who said, "Love your neighbor as yourself." Be kind, patient, and true to your own self first, and then pour out that kindness and the joy of your life to others.

There is one person we can emulate freely, and that is Jesus Christ. So, do to others what you would have them do to you. We want to be encouraged, so encourage. We want to be understood, so understand. We want to be loved, so love. And all of these things will come back around to you, for I know God said, "Cast your bread upon the water and it will return." Be sincere and persistent to become "A New You."

Share the Blessings of Summer Fun

For our older daughter's fifth birthday, her daddy plans to build her a little one's life-size playhouse. I envision this precious dwelling painted light pink, adorned with white shutters. It will have a porch in the front with a small swing and scrolled woodwork, which is called Victorian gingerbread. Inside we will decorate the tiny house with floral printed wallpaper, lace curtains, and tiny pictures. We will paint floral throw rugs on the wooden floors and furnish it with white wicker furniture.

When it is completed, we will have an open house and invite some of our daughter's neighborhood friends and their mommies, too, for a lovely tea party. We will all dress in Victorian hats, long dresses, and gloves, and I'll serve fresh-baked cookies and handpicked strawberries and grapes. What fun!

This summer, enjoy the enchantment of the season by partaking in some of these ideas for summer fun. If you have a little girl or grand-daughter, you might construct a playhouse for her, too. Build a tree house for the boys in the family, as my friend did last summer for her six-year-old grandson. They made a spiral staircase around the tree trunk, leading up to the front door, and spent the night under the stars. You might go camping in a tent in the backyard. Tell stories and eat hot dogs and roast marshmallows over a fire and sing songs.

Try hiking up a mountain trail. Or go canoeing, gliding silently down a beautiful stream, becoming one with God's nature. Being out-doors can refresh and relax you. (Whenever you're outdoors, remember to apply your sunscreen, at least SPF 15, to your face, neck, and body, including the back of your hands, and reapply it often.)

Help the neighborhood kids put up a lemonade stand in front of your house, and be the first and best customer. Make homemade ice cream and invite the people on the block for an ice cream sundae party.

Plant a garden and share your harvest with your friends. Each day watch in wonder as your plants flourish under all of your tender loving care.

Take the children to a farm to pick strawberries. Come home and make strawberry shortcake with lots and lots of whipped cream.

Go to the beach and hunt for perfect shells. Look for starfish and do what one twelve-year-old boy once did. A storm had washed hundreds of starfish up onto the shore. As the young boy walked along the beach, he picked up the starfish one by one and threw them back into the water. A man saw what the boy was doing, came up to him, and said, "What are you doing? There are hundreds of starfish on this beach. Throwing a few back in the water won't make any difference." The boy bent down, picked up another starfish, and said, smiling, "It made a difference to that one."

So remember to make a difference.

Watch the vast and glorious sunset with someone special. It is an original painting from God, for you who love the Master Painter.

Boating is great fun! Try paddleboats that you pedal just like a bicycle; rent a rowboat or a sailboat. Join a bird-watching group and become familiar with God's sweet singers. Learn to identify their songs.

Plant flowers—lots and lots of flowers. Choose colors that delight the eye. These lovely blossoms can inspire you to be more aware of God's tender beauty.

Whatever you do this summer, do it with a joy-filled heart full of thanksgiving. For we are most blessed, and the only thing that we can do to make the blessings better is to share them! Have a wonderful and delightful season.

Be Still and Know That God Is Near

I've heard it said that "The good and the wise lead quiet lives." There is a great secret in this. They are "good" because they trust in God within them. They are "quiet" because they look for Him and listen to Him constantly.

The best time of your life is now . . . now is so full of opportunity to see God, so slow down and realize it!

Time cannot be bought or sold, borrowed or saved, reproduced or modified. We must make the best use of this precious commodity or it will slip away. Now is life.

Pascal said, "One half of the ills of life come because men are unwilling to sit down quietly for thirty minutes to think of all the possible consequences of their actions."

With our hectic lifestyles, it is of utmost importance to stop, for the health of your mind, body, and spirit. Keeping silent gives us the opportunity to hear with the ears of God.

Go outdoors and soak up the glory of nature, which God made. See the leaves of the trees gently waving in the breeze, and be serenaded by the birds. When the birds are not singing, they're so quiet in their work.

Do quiet things. Explore the unknown. Think happy thoughts, work in the garden, or paint a picture. Those creative outlets can relax you. Have a picnic with the little ones in your life. Never lose perspective on what is really important. The sweetest music is in the moments we share with those we love, hearing the joy of their laughter and the tiny words "I love you."

Take a stroll by the seashore; sit and watch the waves rolling in and out in a steady, perpetual rhythm. Consider their boundaries, set by God.

Watch the gulls as they stand on the sand knowing He has supplied all the food they will ever need in that great vast sea. How much more than that will He supply for you? For you are of much more value than the birds.

Sit quietly and consider these things.

In this world of hustle and bustle we need to be reminded of what truly is important in life, which is God and our relationship to Him.

Move everything through God, not man. Lift up your heart and praise Him, give thanks for all of our blessings. The more you praise Him, the more He will do. Feel God's peace within and think on the security and serenity of childhood. Say a prayer of thanksgiving, even if it begins with "God is great, God is good. Let us thank Him for our food." The prayers of God's children go up to Him like the sweet smell of flowers, so as we talk with Him, the fragrance of His love and care are returned to us.

In the still of the night or the dew of the morning, talk with Jesus. He is called the Prince of Peace. Look into His eyes; they are deep wells of security. Every step with God gives you victory over every problem. His quietness holds perfect control, and the Prince of Peace will walk with you.

Be wise; read the instruction book before you start the day. In the Bible are the words that make life work. They will sink down to your subconscious, drop into your heart, and give you inner peace. Now . . . you're living!

Forgive Someone and You'll Feel Better

For your sake, for your peace of mind, for your health's sake, put all your resentments into God's hands and walk away from them, leaving them to His wisdom and will.

Resentment begins an ongoing cycle of hurt with each remembrance of the wrongdoing. Harboring resentment is like hanging on to a virus; you are the only one who feels it, and the other party involved might not even care. For every minute you remain bitter, you lose sixty seconds of peace.

Forgiving heals and helps you. Studies have found that nursing a grudge is hard on your body. Researchers at Hope College in Michigan asked volunteers to think about a time when someone hurt them. When dwelling on their resentment, the subjects showed greater physiological and emotional stress, higher blood pressure and heart rate, and intense facial expressions (lots of wrinkles). When volunteers were told to imagine forgiving the person, they felt happier and in control.

Let go of bitterness. Forget those grievances. Holding a grudge only hurts you. Harboring a hurt steals the joy from your life. It robs you of sleep, health, and contentment. It turns life into drudgery and stains all that is good in you. Resentment twists your personality into something you don't want or like. Your mind begins to feel tired and dull.

In sum, it eradicates love from your heart and makes the Holy Spirit stand far off.

Pray for those who have hurt you. If you bless them instead of cursing them, then you will be free. Give the problem to God. He will work it out to your exceedingly great joy.

Return love for hate. Replace bitterness with compassion,

understanding, and love. Ignore faults; concentrate on what is good. You can't change a person by enumerating their faults. I like to remember what Paul wrote in 1 Corinthians 13:7: "Love bears all things, believes all things, hopes all things, endures all things." So forgive others as you want God to forgive you. Look for the good in one another. We all have faults, and we want others to look for the good in us.

Many of us have been forsaken by so many that it is sometimes hard to believe that someone will be a true friend. But, oh, what a friend we have in Jesus. He is a friend who sticks closer to us than a brother. God is our defense. You may never know how He has vindicated you but He does. Don't rely on human feelings; they are deceiving. Trust in God's unchanging word.

Repentance is the key to happiness. Repentance means to turn around and go the other way. It is important to stop and reflect on our lives every day. If we let our emotions rule us, we become very childish and immature.

What we eat or drink can affect our emotions. Too much caffeine, a lot of fried foods and rich desserts, too much salt—all these things can affect our emotional outlook and cause overreaction.

Therefore, we must consciously decide to bring our actions and reactions into agreement with the Word of God. If God says forgive, then forgive. Let us be obedient to His love. Every command from God is for our good. Don't hold grudges or resentment.

God is love, and His love for us is thorough, even to keeping our bodies healthy and well and our spirits full of His joy.

He came that we might have life and live more abundantly. Let us make each moment shine with love and appreciation, forgetting those things that are behind us and pressing on to giving Him first place with all our heart, mind, and strength. Let our face mirror the joy of knowing we have been forgiven, and so we forgive.

"Simple Gifts" Is More Than a Shaker Song

A child is happy with a simple cardboard box for a creative, imaginary toy.

Be content with whatsoever you have, for I recall that God said, "I will never leave you or forsake you."

A person's life consists of much more than the abundance of things he or she possesses. The good in human life is shown in quiet appreciation of the things money cannot buy.

"The true perfection of man lies not in what man has, but in what man is," wrote Oscar Wilde. You can have a wonderful life measured by the joy you give others.

Real contentment comes from the heart. The sweetness of love, the awareness of a Heavenly Father, and peace of mind are makers of happiness that no condition or amount of land or coin can depress. Money and property will not fill your life with joy. A wise person knows that what's really important in life is giving and receiving love.

Difficult times have helped me to understand how infinitely rich and beautiful life is and that worldly goods and the status symbols that we are bombarded with are of little importance. Material items can be enjoyed; admit them into your life, but never base your happiness on them.

The price one pays for "things" is sometimes so high that in the end these items can become a great loss to you. Honor, integrity, a clear conscience, spending time with a loving family, and good health are just a few treasures beyond any material gain. So the next time you are envious of a coworker's promotion, a neighbor's new boat or fancy car, do not be. To be dissatisfied about what you don't have is to waste the joy in what you do have. Earthly things never satisfy.

"For what shall it profit a man if he gain the whole world and suffer the loss of his soul."—Mark 8:36.

Simplify your life. Lighten your burdens. Take pleasure in the little joys: the freshly fallen snow, the sound of beautiful music, or a warm cup of cocoa and a good book. These are graces free to all. In the most humble places, you will find these jewels.

The person who is richest is the one who is happy with the least and shares the most. Stop for a moment and take a look at true wealth, such as genuine character, trusted friendships, and self-respect. These are priceless attributes.

Concentrate on all the wonderful qualities that you possess. You have so much. What really matters is the love that is eternal. Share your love and your blessings with others. Offer to run errands for a busy mom, help a neighbor shovel his walkway, or bake cookies for a shut-in. You will find that you are rich indeed.

It is a paradox that true wealth is found not in how much you have, but in how much you can give away. You have a wealth of very needful gifts within you . . . a smile, a pat on the back, a compliment, a word of encouragement, or a few moments to listen with a caring heart.

I know someone who said that, when money was scarce, for special occasions her family gave each other "tickets" that they created—coupons to wash the dishes, cook dinner, fold the laundry, or wash the car. These "tickets" made heartwarming gifts.

The greatest treasure is already yours: life itself, and the freedom to choose to walk and talk with God and to know the depths and height of His love.

Don't Delay; Make Exercise Part of Your Routine

"I'll start my diet tomorrow." "Someday, I'll begin that fitness routine." "I don't have time to exercise or eat right." These are familiar phrases most of us have said at one time or another . . . or say all the time!

But we can break the bad habits by discovering a power within. You have the ability to change your life or to turn it around. You have far greater potential than you can imagine and can gain victory by knowing that the miracle is in you. See yourself as the magnificent individual that you are, caring so much about your health and well-being that you start the good habit of good health.

So let's not put it off till tomorrow. Let's start today! It is just the beginning of "A New You," looking and feeling years younger, slim, and confident. Believe in yourself. If you are willing to work hard, nothing is impossible. The countless rewards will be worth the sacrifices. (Just remember, you should always consult your doctor before beginning any fitness or nutrition program.)

Do some form of exercise every day. It can help to reduce depression, stress, and mental clutter, while increasing awareness, energy, and relaxation. Write down workouts on your calendar as if they were business appointments. That way you'll be less likely to break them. Try exercising with a friend to keep you motivated. Pick activities that you enjoy so you'll be more apt to stick with it. To head off excuses, keep a gym bag packed in the car for an after-work workout.

Exercise first thing in the morning for a great way to start your day and to leave you feeling energized. Sneak in exercise during your lunch hour. Get in active, quality time with your family by hiking, skating, or biking together. Even everyday tasks can be done energetically.

This is the simplest diet of all: Eliminate all sweets, except fruits, and substitute low-fat for high-fat foods. Cut down on butter, cheese, fatty meats, sour cream, and ice cream. Fat should be the smallest portion of your diet.

Avoid salt and salty foods. Take the salt shaker off of the table and the stove. Season with fresh black pepper and dried spices and herbs.

Eat fewer processed foods. Nutrition experts recommend emphasizing complex carbohydrates as your energy base. Such foods include whole grains, vegetables, cereal, stone-ground breads, brown rice, and fruits. Add beans to your soups and salads as your protein source. Seek variety in your diet to be sure you're getting the full range of vitamins and minerals you need. Try experimenting with a new recipe each week.

Be sure you drink water before and after your workout and throughout the day. Dehydration can reduce your energy and your exercise performance. A cool eight-ounce glass of water will cut your desire to binge in half.

Don't compare yourself with others. Everyone shapes up at his or her own rate. Your goal should be a healthy body, and with it a radiant glow, an inner confidence, and a sense of well-being.

Give yourself a reward for not giving up. Cheer on your successes with lots of TLC.

Once you have experienced the positive effects of exercising, healthy eating, and the exhilaration afterward, you'll know you can achieve anything! Just knowing that other people have successfully lost weight and kept it off by exercising can give you the inspiration that you can, too. And I will be so proud of you!

Rushing Everywhere Takes Us Further from God

Every soul is a precious prize and wears a stamp across it that says "Top Priority." You are top priority to God, and also top priority to the enemy.

I read in the Bible, "To whom you yield your body's members, he it is whose servant you are." My heart's desire is to make the number-one priority on my list my relationship with God. The number-one priority on the enemy's list is to keep me from deepening my experience with the Lord.

How the enemy does this is by keeping me so busy, busy, busy, waving things that need to be done in front of me constantly. The enemy wants to steal our time. To throw every distraction in our way so we never get down to business with God.

How busy are you? Engaged in rushing here and there, occupied with nonessentials that in the long run really mean nothing? Hustling and bustling with little inspirations to do this or that, immersing your intellect in politics, using all your energy to run business, home, and leisure time? Between careers and family, children and pets, errands and housework, friends and acquaintances, cars and trains, we have not a second to ourselves to simply just sit next to God and lean on His calming, strengthening, awesome shoulder.

In the busyness of life, we need to do this much more than we realize. There is nothing, absolutely nothing, more important to do. And nothing that is so subtly sidetracked.

I'm so guilty of this myself, with work at the office and work at home that occupies nearly every waking moment. As soon as I take an instant to stop and pray or read a sermon, the thought comes: "You better do this," or "Get that done before . . . . "

"So what shall we do about it?" one may ask. Realize what it is that we put as top priority in our lives. There is no doubt that we obviously have our daily food up there on the top three. Why do we make time to eat at least two or three meals a day? Because the hunger pain of our body demands it. What about the hunger pain of our souls? It is the essence of our eternal being—that still, small longing for greater love and peace, a nobler reason for living, and a security beyond the rise and fall of the stock market or even our nation.

If each day we could give God a thirty-minute or one-hour span of time that we take to feed our body and let Him feed our souls, our lives would be turned around. Instead of looking downward over a desk, look up at Him, at His expression of beauty around us and into His eyes. Our souls would be refreshed and satisfied. We would be conquerors of busyness and victors of life.

We all need to learn that life is too short and precious to waste. This time we have on earth is incredibly short compared to eternity. I recall that Job said, "Man is like the grass or a flower that blooms in the morning and in a few days faded away."

I have a friend who told me of a certain rose that she still remembers seeing five years ago. For a moment she was caught up in its beauty, and God let her see its glory in its depths. It was so pure, white, and sweet, and its fragrance filled the air around it. Looking at the rose was like looking, for an instant, at the robe Jesus was enfolded in. He was enfolded in the beauty of that rose for that moment. Of such experience is the kingdom of Heaven.

I want my life to be like that rose—to drink in God's beauty and give it out to the world to see a little bit of Him. To refresh the weary travelers, to lift up the downcast and give all a glimpse of eternity. But I must take time to spend alone with Him in order to reflect the loveliness of our Heavenly Father.

Part Three
SPIRIT

*"I have held many things in my hands
and I have lost them all; But whatever I
placed in God's hands, that I still possess."*
—Martin Luther

He Is There, Especially in the Darkest Moments

In the examining room, two parents and their six-year-old son sat quietly as the surgeon spoke. "In the morning I will open your son's heart . . . " Interrupting, the little boy said quickly with a light shining in his eyes, "You'll find Jesus there."

The surgeon looked up in shock and then continued. "I will see how much damage has been done and then . . . " Again the boy said, "You'll find Jesus there. He lives in my heart." With a slight frown the surgeon stated to the parents, "I'm sure there are weakened vessels, low blood supply, and damaged muscles. When I operate, we will hope for the best." And with that he left the room.

The surgeon then went back to his office. Sitting down at his desk, he looked again at the little boy's records and x-rays. "Why?" asked the surgeon. "Why do these things happen?" Then, turning to God for the first time in his life, he asked, "Why have you brought this little boy here for such a short time? You made him. You created his weak heart. Why?"

Then, to his great surprise, the surgeon felt the awesome presence of God speak deep within his own heart. "The boy belongs to me and he is my lamb and his purpose on earth is accomplished. He has retrieved for me another lamb and he will come back into my arms and his parents will follow later."

Such a great revelation of God's love enveloped the surgeon that he put his head down on his desk and wept.

After surgery, the worried parents sat with the surgeon by the boy's hospital bed. When the lad awoke, he looked at the surgeon wearily and asked, "Did you cut open my heart?" The surgeon replied, "Yes, son."

"What did you find?" whispered the boy.

With joy and tears in his eyes, the surgeon said, "I found Jesus there . . . and He found me."

If you seek God with all your heart, you will surely find Him.

The grasses of the field bend and bow with the tempestuous wind. Though which force is stronger? That which comes against us, or the ability to humbly bow and let it pass?

When the winds of adversity blow, then is the time to bow before God and know Him.

I know that God has perfect control in this universe, and all things work together for good for those who love Him and are called according to His purpose.

I find that if I pray and give all my problems to God, they will become an accomplishment as He directs, for all things become precious as we seek to live in His will.

We must take our trials with the grace to know it is the hand of the Heavenly Sculptor that allows the blow to the marble, knowing that the beauty within is about to be revealed. There is nothing more beautiful in life than knowing our great loving Father is preparing us for life in His kingdom. For only perfect beauty, which is perfect love, can enter there. Let Him shape your life. Yield with love to His love, which oftentimes comes in disguise.

I tell my little ones that once the lights go out in a room, it seems so incredibly dark, but as we wait, holding hands, things begin to appear and we can see them take shape. The children and I know, as blind Fanny Crosby wrote, "Standing somewhere in the shadows we'll find Jesus. He's the one who always cares and understands."

And I say to them, "Yes, my little darlings, through all life's dark trials . . . Jesus is there."

Humble Yourself and You Will Be Lifted Up

Whenever you are disappointed with your spot in life, remember Sarah.

As a little schoolgirl, Sarah auditioned for a part in the school play but was not picked to be in the cast. Instead of being upset or bitter, Sarah told her mother with full excitement, "I was chosen to clap and cheer for my schoolmates!"

Those words and that attitude have made her admirable. No matter what our position, we are of vital importance to others around us . . . and to God.

Humbleness of heart is a beautiful quality. It brings such contentment and a closer walk with God. The proud ones will have a hard time getting along in life, for they will always meet with constant competition; there will always be someone more talented, beautiful, and rich. But those who are humble develop a character that draws true friends and quiet, steady achievement. "Humble yourself in the sight of the Lord and He shall lift you up."—James 4:10.

We all have experienced being talked down to and looked down upon, and we can begin to believe it until we hear the voice within saying, " I have special, individual plans for you." There are no two fingerprints alike. You are a unique creation.

By the Word of God, get into action and do what you have been wishing to do. God squeezes us into hard places so we can prove to ourselves that we have the faith, determination, and persistence to succeed with other people.

In order to overcome, you must humbly place yourself in another person's shoes. If you understand yourself and others, you will achieve great wisdom. True consideration for another and humble obedience to the Word of God will make your life glorious.

Stop expecting from others what you can only get from God. Sometimes life can be an uphill battle because we do not just have peaks, but have many valleys. More than anything, when you are in either one, you have to praise God that much more, for He is the One who will get you through them all.

If you're looking to another person for your source of fulfillment, perfect love, or happiness, you can hang up life. It cannot be found in any other person. Realize that everyone has imperfections and it's all right. So tap into God's wisdom and perfect love. If you want love, security, and wisdom in all that you do . . . go to God first.

If you are a janitor, maid, or chief executive officer, be the absolute best that you can be. Whatever you do in word or deed, do it as unto the Lord. God has given many a janitor or maid the wisdom to invest wisely, so that they have left a six-figure legacy to family and community. God has given many a CEO the wisdom to be content and blessed because they humbled themselves enough to get on their knees and take it all to God, to really care about the personal lives of the staff, janitors, and maids, letting the joy of a sincere "thank-you" and pat on the back encourage others.

The more you look to God, the more you can make your paths straight again and full of promise. Our delight should be like His delight. His delight is to make things right, to give us complete joy and peace, and make others happy. He continually cares and is gladdened to lift you up.

No matter how humble our position, do it well . . . and God will clap and cheer for you!

God Shows His Love Through Nature

God loves to surround us with many wonderful things. From daylight to dark, over the pastures, hills, and valley, we see His beautiful expression of resurrection in the spring.

When we look upon nature, we experience tenderness within, an awesome awareness of the grandeur and infinite beauty of God's character.

"Lord, help me to teach my children about You," I prayed as we walked amongst the trees. Just then, in a blink of an eye, a beautiful butterfly flew by. That was my answer.

Nature is God's love letter to us. There is so much to learn from the world that surrounds us. Each sunrise is a reminder of His glorious creativity as the curtain of night rises and the spotlight of the sun dances on the leaves with drops of dew. Pink and purple crocuses peeking through the recently thawed soil are a sign of God's faithfulness to keep life safe and warm even through the cold winter.

Watch the squirrels. They are such hard workers. On a fall day they don't sit around or rest. They instinctively know the cold days are coming and food will be scarce, so they gather their food and store it up so when the snow comes and is piled high, they will have plenty to eat and be warm. The wise squirrels teach us to plan ahead and not be slothful.

Consider the ants. These busy creatures persistently build, gather, and store. The ants, some naturalists observed, seem to have a rule among them: If an ant doesn't work, that ant doesn't eat. We all must do our part, and then we can all partake.

See the birds singing joyously as they diligently fly here and there, gathering twigs or straw to build their nests. Each puts its nest in just the right place to guard it during the storms. During breaks in their work, they stop to give thanks and sing their praises to God.

The eagle flies higher than any bird. It's powerful and brave as it sets its gaze into the heavens, soars above this busy world, and finds his shelter in the cleft of the rock. So we must be like the eagle, setting our sights on heaven and finding our safety at the crucified side of Jesus Christ, where we are saved from all the attacks of the enemy.

The perfect example of how even the tiniest bit of faith can make great changes is the little acorn as it grows into the mighty oak tree. All the trees lift their arms in praise, as our hearts should be lifted to God in prayer continually.

And then, of course, there is the weeping willow. This tree shows us the beauty in sorrow as we humbly bow and ask God to let His perfect will be done. For we know that He is a healer and a solver of every problem.

A friend once told me that as a child, she remembered looking up in the sky and searching for God. Even then she had a longing deep within to know His great love. And without a doubt, He has answered that longing, as He will for anyone who comes to Him with childlike faith. Christ within us is amazing, a living well within our souls, bubbling up, flowing out, and refreshing others.

God can strip away all the pain of yesteryear. He makes us new, just as nature sparkles with colors after the raging storm has swept away all the dead leaves and limbs. Nature renews itself season after season; it witnesses the promise that God is continually at work on the landscapes of our lives, planting His Word in our hearts.

When my little girl bends down and with wonder looks at a flower, I kneel down and meet those sweet little eyes shining with complete faith as she says, "Mommy, God made this flower." I hug her with responding joy and say, "Yes, my darling, it is so beautiful, just like He is." And as Genesis 9:16 states, "Whenever the rainbow appears in the clouds, I will see it and remember the everlasting covenant between God and all living creatures of every kind on the earth."

A Time to Pray May Be Found Late at Night

Lately, I've been awakening at three every morning. Sometimes, the sky is filled with a multitude of bright, shining stars, but most often the soft clouds cover the moon. Gone is the hustle and bustle of the day. Still and silent, the world sleeps.

A friend of mine said, "I think God is calling you to special prayer." And I think she was right. Since then, I have spent those quiet moments with Him so He can pour more of Himself into my heart and strengthen me for the day ahead. Then, I can pass on to you, dear readers, the sweet treasures of His storehouse of wisdom. It is only after I rest in Him that I am able to once again fall into a deep and healing sleep.

The Old Testament tells us that at 6 P.M., 9 P.M., midnight, and 3 A.M., men turned to God to pray. This was called the "night watch," a time of communication with God. If you find yourself awakened in the middle of the night, I know that the Bible says, "Do not be anxious about anything, but in everything, by prayer and petition, with thanksgiving, present your requests to God."

I would start with giving thanks. Besides presenting the greatest matters in life, take the little or trivial things also to God. If something keeps you awake at night, immediately turn to Him. Search your heart, and if you find that something is disturbing your peace of mind, look to the Father and you will be restored to calm.

Speak to the Lord about anything that may be troubling you: a trial you may be facing, a business problem, or family issue. Remember, you are God's masterpiece, and your life is your masterpiece. You are a beautiful sculpture molded of the clay of the dust of the earth. If for some reason it has become marred, just go to God and He will take hold of your heart and remold it again and give you a clean start.

He is the problem solver, the dissolver of doubts, and the giver of dreams that can hold the solutions. I have found something that will replace the need of sleeping pills in a hurry. Pick up your Bible to read in bed; it's a foolproof way to conquer insomnia. I believe when we open up the Word of God, angels crowd near. And when we speak to Him, our worries and cares disappear and He gives us songs in the night.

Be patient with God. He is so patient with you, waiting throughout your life for you to understand what great love and forgiveness He has for you.

"I remember my mother saying, 'Hang in there. God is never in a hurry, He is never late, and always there.' I find it all so true," says an eighty-five-year-old lady. Eighty-five years is quite enough time to prove God's presence and see the outcome of His loving purpose for you. He is always there, any hour of the night or day.

Every individual in the world has his or her own personality or spirit. In the middle of the day, you can feel the press and jostling of millions of spirits running to and fro after this or that. How peaceful it is when God lets them fall asleep and the night becomes so still. I can almost hear Him breathe a great sigh of relief. Then He bends down and hovers over someone He wants to talk to, someone He loves, someone He wants to reveal the treasures of His heart to.

One of the most glorious things I know of is to wake in the middle of the dark night and hear a single bird singing its heart out to God. Let us imitate nature in the night watch. After our requests are known, let us sing our hearts out in praise to a very precious, loving Heavenly Father.

God Is Invisible, Yet He Is Always There

*I*f He resides in your heart, He is enthroned in your life and glorified in your actions.

Take hold of God's hand. Even though you cannot physically see it, it is there. You may not be able to hear Him, yet He can speak through your voice. And you cannot physically touch God, but He is the power that gives you life.

When you need Him, He is there. Even if you deny Him, He will never deny that He has said, "I am with you always." When you feel alone, He is beside you. In your tears or fears, He is there. Trust in an all-wise and powerful Father. With God there is a peace, an assurance that you can cling to, and a love that never leaves you. All that He allows in your life is for your good.

The Lord has a unique plan for you, a divine purpose. Seek Him and you will discover it is so. In absolute stillness, absorb the Lord's permeating peace and His miraculous works. Being aware of Him brings rest. Listen to His still, small voice within you. To obey is to find the answers. I remember that the Bible says, "Greater is He that is within you than the enemy in the world."

God's presence cannot be absorbed by talking of or taking part in the devil's works or tricks. The enemy wants to upset us and stifle our creativity, but we can overcome by learning his tactics, handling conflicts calmly, and praying for God's wisdom.

The devil has no new thoughts, just new people to work through. The inner quality of self-control can help to let God's thoughts take over. God is full of new ideas and creativity. So let your confidence be in God. He has the final say. The joy of the Lord is like ammunition. It defeats the enemy every time. Don't be discouraged by criticism, just pray that God will touch the heart and soul of those who criticize.

Those who comfort with a helping hand, who encourage with praise, and love with God's love, defeat the enemy every time. May you be blessed by remembering who you are.

We are sons and daughters of the magnificent King—wonderfully made creations that God put on this earth not to be victims, but victorious. What a beautiful quality you have, dear reader, to be able to humble yourself enough to learn from God's wisdom. It is a gift that begets greatness. Read His textbook; become a heavenly student.

We are in a battle, and the battlefield is in our minds. Don't let the enemy's thoughts remain there. You can't stop the enemy from launching negative thoughts like missiles into your mind, but you can send up an anti-missile of God's Word and blow it up before it makes a scar. Then just refuse to keep on thinking about the problem. At the end of a trying day, leave all of it behind you as you put your mind on Psalm 4:8: "I will both lay me down in peace, and sleep: for thou, Lord, only makes me dwell in safety."

When you eliminate negativity, malice, and strife, I believe angels gather around and rejoice with you. Don't cheat yourself of that time of rejoicing over victory won. Drink in the smiles of the five-star general, Jesus. With His congratulatory arm around your shoulders, walk out on the balcony of life and look over at the setting sun.

In the cool of the evening, have you ever heard the dove's sweet coo? The words I imagine as a backdrop for that precious bird's sound is from John 17, which says, "I in thee . . . thee in me." "I in thee . . . thee in me."

This is the greatest desire He has.

And the love that we share is from Him, dear readers, and therefore it is a love that is eternal. Rest in the knowledge that we are never alone; there are always we three: Him . . . you . . . and me.

Coincidences May Just Be God's Doing

Was it just a coincidence . . . or God's hand? I choose to believe the latter.

I was suddenly awakened at three-thirty in the morning by a disturbing dream. In the dream, we had left the door to our house unlocked. Groggily, I sat up in our darkened room and recalled that earlier that evening we had gone out to the store, and I questioned myself if we had remembered to lock the door when we came home.

I woke up my husband and said, "I just had a strange dream. Did we lock the door?"

He got up, went downstairs, and found the door unlocked.

God cares about us individually and intimately. Many people have said that they believe in God, but that He is too big to be concerned about each little person. I don't think so.

Let me put it this way. There is a little tiny baby, about 17 inches long, and the set of parents, one 6 feet, 4 inches, and the other 5 feet, 7 inches. Do you think those parents are too big to care about their little 17-inch-long baby? Of course not—that baby becomes their whole world. At the smallest whimper, one of those giant parents gets up out of a deep sleep and is at that baby's side in a second. To think that God is any less a parent to His children than we are to ours is ridiculous.

Let us consider God and realize that He who hung the worlds in space and calculated the distances between them so perfectly that life on earth could be sustained for centuries can surely break into our subconscious and let us know to lock the door . . . because God also sees the thief coming up the road.

Nothing happens by chance; there is a divine plan for every day and every circumstance in our lives. God, who is rich in mercy, is nothing but love, comfort, and courage to we who believe. We don't have to be afraid. If we but ask, He holds our hand and helps us through every obstacle. Our Lord will move the world for His children.

We have not because we ask not. Though sometimes God does not give us what we ask for because He knows that down the road, it could bring disaster. I have a friend who is sixty-one years old. She says that most of her prayers are to ask God that only His perfect will be done in the lives of her family and friends. After she is finished praising God for what a wonderful Father He is and how He supplies all her needs, she tells Him that she loves Him for the beauty of His great character and the creation through which He expresses Himself. My friend can only ask for His perfect will to be done, because it is the very best for each individual life from an all-knowing God.

When we plant a garden, do we then go away and not look at it again until harvest time? Of course not. We check it each day, we put a fence around it to keep the rabbits out, pull the weeds so that they will not sap the life from the soil, and water our garden when it gets dry. Does God care any less for us? Never.

I admit it's sometimes a little tough when He pulls the weeds out of my life, but then God hedges me about with His arms of love as I pray and read His Word, and He waters me with refreshing joy as I praise and trust Him.

There are no coincidences with God. And, as the refiner of silver, He sits and watches over me and my house by day and night . . . because He never sleeps or slumbers.

God Stands with Us Now and Forever

We begin to tell when enough is enough. And we become determined not to live in fear. God is our defense. He promised He wouldn't give us more than we can bear, and He never forsakes His own.

Be confident in God's love and let nothing deter you. He wants to build character in you so that you will become strong in the Lord and fear nothing.

Keep your feet planted firmly on higher ground. Place all worries, cares, and woes in God's mighty hands. He will deliver you, give you strength and courage. Go in peace, never be afraid, God will be with you.

If your faith is steadfast, you know that He will guide you in all that you do. He is omnipresent, watching, and He gives His angels charge over us.

We fight the enemy all the time. But we can overcome that enemy and get the victory by faith.

God hears us all at once all over the world regardless of language. He is in control. And part of our character is self-control. We have this because we have faith in Him.

Never ponder over negative thoughts. The older we become, the more we realize that the battleground is in the mind; but if you understand it, you become the victor and peace reigns.

Roman Emperor Marcus Aurelius said, "We become what our thoughts indicate day by day."

The whole world acknowledges this truth, so think on what is good, pure, lovely, and just. Don't let your emotions rule you. Do not be governed by your disappointments. Rise above them with wondrous and new plans for stepping onto higher ground. Remember, God never gives grace for imaginary troubles, but He always gives grace for reality.

There will always be critics, those who think you don't have what it takes, who hurtfully scorn you and talk about you. No matter someone's age, social status, or relationship to you, there are those who can't control the green-eyed monster of envy. Ignore them. Your life is much too valuable to be bothered by this group of small-minded individuals who rarely say a good thing about anyone, who are the first to gossip and to criticize and are jealous. Avoid people who make you unhappy. Hate poisons the soul.

Put yourself in the company of those dear people who genuinely care about you, who are truthful, loyal, and are sincerely considerate. Birds of a feather flock together.

I choose to sit on the line with those who sing from Psalm 106:1, "Give thanks to the Lord, for He is good; His mercy endures forever," then soar into the glorious heavens.

God's love for you never changes. He is everywhere. All you need to do is open your heart and listen.

A reader wrote via e-mail, "People are so busy and totally involved with their own lives that giving a compliment or saying something nice to someone gets left unsaid. One compliment to someone can do wonders."

This will lift you far above the common world and enable you to be like those little birds, spending most of your life above all the confusion and strife. Life is a precious gift, and we should pass the gift of encouragement to others.

Take charge with all that is within you. Saturate your mind with lovely and good things and then act upon them.

Begin every precious day with a prayer of thanksgiving to God and a request to be guided to help one person that day to know that you care . . . because God cares.

Inner Radar Is God's Gift to His Flock

There are flocks upon flocks of sheep in the field. All of a sudden, for no apparent reason, one sheep looks up. Then another sheep lifts its head, and then another . . . and yet another. Almost instinctively, the sheep sense trouble.

And sure enough, totally unseen and creeping up slowly in the distance, there is a hungry and ferocious wolf.

God-given intuition is like a light, a flame of knowledge that gives a warning from the soul, a warning that saves many who in wisdom heed it.

Experience has led me to know that within, God has given me the gift of discernment, which allows me to sense the real objective and instinctively know the purpose people have within their heart. That is, an eye that sees through the outer actions and an ear that hears the motive behind the word.

On one side, goodness and truth sweeten the atmosphere with loveliness as it gathers the aroma of a creative life, as fragrant roses capture the sun. At other times, I can feel the heaviness in the air that surrounds me if it is tainted with jealousy, envy, and strife.

This inner radar, I believe, is God's gift to His children. We must be sensitive to its leading and stop, look, and listen, and always pray, pray, pray.

In the world today, the forces of good and evil are ever prevalent. It is so important to guard your heart, your dear loved ones, and your precious home. Be careful in whom you confide and trust, or you could lose everything. If something within your heart says, "Wait just a minute, something is not quite right," then pause, stand back, and let God be your guide. Read the instruction book of life, the Bible, and talk it over with Him. Wait on God to tell your heart what to do. And if He tells you to remain and do nothing, then do nothing, and be sure . . . He is doing something about your situation.

God guards the homes and hearts of loved ones when you live for Him. When you make a place for God and praise Him, He will come and live there. You will be amazed how He handles the difficult, uncomfortable situations in which you find yourself. When that God-given instinct says, "Wait," then wait . . . days or weeks or even months before you react. God sometimes has to arrange a lot of different people's thinking and even locations before He clears the way and brings about the desired results that will keep you safe in His peace. Just keep your mind fixed on God's power to control the universe. And be aware of all the unseen angels He has placed at your side, in your office, at the entrance of your home, and surrounding your loved ones. Delight yourself in this fact continually and consciously.

Pick out one or two verses in the Bible that strike your heart and repeat them all through the day. Soon, those passages will become part of you. Now, doesn't that inner voice and intuition tell you, "That's right," "That is good," "That is God," "Do it"?

I like to remember that God has said, "I will not leave you comfortless, I will come again and I will be with you, even in you." As we trust in His wonderful words, dear readers, we find that He is in us . . . in the simplicity of that magnificent still, small voice within.

God's Word Is the Only Road Map Needed

"Look at what I have given to you . . . ," the Lord whispered to my heart. "All that you asked for I have given." "Trust yourself and trust Me."

The rejected one, the worthless one, cast out . . . the school of hard knocks was my teacher. But when the heart persists and the desire is right, God gives the victory. You must remember, though, that God can discern the thoughts and intents of the heart.

As I travel on this road of life, there are trials at every turn. The only way I cannot get lost is that I hold up the Word of God in faith. It is my map, it is my rest stop, and it is my place to refuel for the fight. Just as the soldiers planted their flag in the ground when they won a battle, saying, "This land was conquered for this country," God's Word is my banner. It is my absolute.

Living by faith is joyful and victorious. Faith can build an iron wall around you taller than the highest star. It can be perfect safety. Faith comes from the heart and a revelation of Jesus' great love. I know the Bible says, "No weapon formed against you will prosper." With God by your side, nothing can touch you. With Him there is a power greater than all the armies in the world put together. A heavenly host protects you.

Don't be afraid. Having perfect faith means we do not have to worry about whatever the future holds. Let's all work to get to the point where we can say, "My God supplies all of my needs. He has in the past and He will in the future."

God does not exist in time. He is always now. When you speak His Word, He is there to back you up. Your heart grasps the promise and your faith holds it fast; it persists and doesn't give up.

We know we are in a battle and that there is an enemy observing. But remember, you have the whole armor of God. You are a knight in the King's army, so consciously put on that armor every day. First the helmet of salvation, knowing you are saved, which guards your head and your mind. Then, put on the breastplate of righteousness, which guards your heart. His righteousness makes you worthy. Gird your loins with the truth, knowing deep within you what is right. Prepare your feet to walk in that Gospel.

On your arm carry the shield of faith, whereby you will stop all the fiery darts of the wicked. And above all (and you must study it to know how to handle it), carry the sword of the spirit, which is the Word of God, for with it you will cut the enemy to ribbons.

If the enemy delivers a situation that you feel you cannot handle, put it in God's hands. He will defend and vindicate you in His time. Do not lose any sleep over the adverse situation.

Trust and rest. God is only a prayer away. Pray that the proper resolution will come to pass. Ask the Lord for help in dealing with any issue. Before long He will work these things around for your good. I like to recall that the Bible says, "Before they call I will answer." He knows what you need and has already started the solution. Adversity makes you who you are. You don't develop fine character by sitting on a soft pillow; you get it from walking on hard rocks.

Give thanks always. Being thankful activates the zeal of God for His children to be the victors and to make it happen. Life isn't a smooth sail; it's hard work to crest the great waves of stormy seas. But always remember this: We can wake the Lord of glory with our cries, and He will arise and put His foot on the rail of our boat and say with a voice that all the universe must obey, "Peace, be still . . . ," and so we are.

Still, quiet, and safe.

If It Looks Like a Snake, It Probably Is

There was once a slithering snake trying to cross a busy road. A young lady was passing by merrily when the snake saw her and said, "Please, nice lady, pick me up and carry me across the street."

The lady looked at him doubtfully. "But you're a snake; you'll bite me."

And the snake replied, sugary sweet, "Oh no, I won't hurt you. I just want to get to the other side."

The lady cautiously answered, "I can't . . . I really don't think I can."

The snake replied, "Pretty please, I promise I won't bite you. I know you are so nice. I know you will do it for poor little me," he said slyly.

So, the lady slowly lifted up the snake and carried him across the street. Just as they got to the other side, the snake bit her horribly.

"Why did you bite me?" the lady cried. "You said you wouldn't harm me!"

"You knew I was a s-s-s-snake . . . ," he sneered at her and laughed, " . . . once a s-s-s-snake, always a s-s-s-snake."

Use caution when entrusting your heart to others. No matter how nice some are, be wise. The Bible tells us to beware of wolves in sheeps' clothing, so weigh matters carefully before taking action.

I have received many letters from trusting people who have lost money, careers, and hearts to unworthy causes. I am not talking about giving up trust completely, but I am talking about taking every encounter to the only wise and true God first. Then give yourself time in prayer and read the Word of God. In the Bible is great wisdom and caution. Especially in Proverbs, where King Solomon, considered the wisest monarch the world has ever known, has written down the wisdom given to him by God.

For when God called Solomon to be king, he was just a young boy of about sixteen. Solomon was so awed by this great position of being a ruler of Israel and over thousands of people, that he begged God for wisdom to know how to rule over his inheritance.

God was so pleased with this unselfish and humble request that He gave Solomon not only the wisdom asked for, but also wealth beyond description, grandeur, honor, and peace in his kingdom for all of his days. I know Proverbs 2:10–12 says, "When wisdom enters your heart . . . discretion shall preserve you and understanding will keep you to deliver you from evil men." So put those wonderful words to memory. There are no greater words of wisdom than those found in the Bible. They will help you to avoid all kinds of problems and mistakes that you would regret later. Putting these promises into practice is a perfect way of proving how true and wise they really are.

I think of my innocent and sweet baby daughters growing up, and I reflect upon all of the young men and women just entering college. And I so desire to implant discretion and wisdom in their hearts. There is so much temptation offered to them in the disguise of charm, beauty, and false promises. There is only one true advice that I can give. Get very close to God. Read your Bible and pray, pray, pray. For wisdom will protect and deliver you.

We are bringing our children up, at their very young age, to talk to God. To thank Him at every meal, to guide their pursuits of the day, and at night to place in His hands their safety while they sleep . . . and to pray that their Heavenly Father will give them wisdom for life.

Do Not Be Afraid; God Stands by You Always

*T*here is no fear with God by your side. Abolish fear and you can accomplish anything you wish. God is always with those who rejoice in Him, for He inhabits the praises of His people.

"God is with you," a dear friend said to me as I agonized over a situation. "Do not worry. Every trial is an opportunity for God to show what a mighty deliverer He is."

Things seem to hit all at once. How difficult it is when trials come—stress upon stress, worry upon worry—when your stomach is sick with tension. This situation happens to everyone. You are awake all night with anxiety, and your nerves are raw. Rest and do not worry. If you call upon Him, you will realize you will be fine. God is with you.

I was experiencing great anxiety; everything seemed to overwhelm me. Looking for direction in my dilemma, I opened up my Bible randomly to Ezekiel, Chapter 36. I began to read, "Be aware, I am for you and I will turn unto you. I will settle you and I will do better for you than at your beginning. And you shall know I am the Lord. I will put my spirit within you and cause you to walk in my words and you shall keep my judgments and do them and you shall be my people and I will be your God.

"Then the heathen that are left round about you shall know that I the Lord build ruined places, and plant that which was desolate. I the Lord have spoken it, and I will do it."

A calm came over my entire being and I felt the Lord saying to me, "I am here and I am your defense."

Be strong in the Lord when crises arise. God is for you and He will provide all His angels to protect you. Always have faith in what He does, even though its beginnings are invisible to your eyes. When He hears the cries of His people saying, "Heavenly Father, look what they are doing . . . help me," He whispers in our hearts, "I am delighted to show myself strong on your behalf." God does not stand for the heathen; He will defend you against them.

I read in the Bible of King Hezekiah, who proudly displayed all his treasures before another king, whom he really did not know. This king became his enemy, for he was jealous of Hezekiah and wanted to destroy him. The jealous king took advantage of the knowledge of the treasures and came back later with a strong army, besieged the city, and took all the treasures for himself.

We are here to learn from this example and guard our treasures at all costs. Be forewarned and careful in whom you trust. Even someone who approaches you with a hand of friendship could unmercifully turn on you. A brother can deceive you, or business associates might put a knife in your back.

If situations happen that upset you, know that God will deliver you and give you abundantly more. Have faith when you don't understand, for God said He would work it together for good. You will be safe and your family protected.

When God takes away something, He always gives in its place something better. Second Peter 1:4 says, "Whereby are given unto us exceeding great and precious promises." God guides your every decision, shields you with His strength, and surrounds you with His love. His promise to you is strong and sure. God provides shelter in the midst of storms.

The reward for a person's toil is not what they get for it in terms of monetary value, but what they become by it. Albert Schweitzer said, "One who gains strength by overcoming obstacles possesses the only strength which can overcome adversity."

The joy of the Lord is our strength. Invest that fact within your heart, and nothing on earth can take it away. It comes from the Word of God, and it is eternal.

God Is with Us

Long before I was old enough to understand why, I knew that God was always with me, guiding me and directing my footsteps.

One summer when I was a little girl, my mother and I were at the beach on the New Jersey shoreline. Mother, who loved the water, was a good swimmer and moved in the water with comfort and ease. She swam in the bright blue seas happily, while I, at just six years old, had gotten only my feet wet as I merrily played close to shore.

Suddenly and without warning, the sun disappeared and the sky turned dark. Crashing waves looked sky-high and the winds blew sand into my eyes. In the ocean's vastness, I started calling out, "Mom? Mommy, where are you?" I heard not a voice. Again, I screamed, "Mommy! Mommy!"

Through the undertow of the waves, I saw her straining to swim to shore. I was shoulder-deep into the water, as I tried desperately to reach her. The waves kept pulling Mother farther and farther back into the ocean's roar.

Finally, with outstretched arms, my hand touched hers and we both dragged ourselves onto the sandy beach. The rocks had cut her legs from the many times the current pulled her underwater as she strained to reach me. But we were safe. I was shaking and shivering from fright, and my mother held me tightly in her arms and calmly said, "Don't worry, my child, God is with us."

There have been many times, even now that I am grown, that I have felt like that little, frightened girl on the beach. But the good Lord has always shown me the way. And I still know that God is always, always with us.

I know now that the difficulties we face are like the sharp rocks and the ocean's undertow. But by taking my mother's advice not to worry,

I find that they can be used as stepping stones of God's grace to carry me onto the place where God desires me to be. God is the only safe harbor from the storms of life. I know if I leave my problems to the Lord, things will work out.

In Him I have found the greatest joy, the indescribable blessedness of my existence. The realization that He is with me everywhere is one of the most glorious facts of my life.

During challenging times, I know that this turbulence is necessary to develop strength of character. What does the stormy sea do? It brings up all the flotsam and jetsam of useless things and casts it out. Difficulties help me to know what I consider not important in life, to cast it out and to take hold of unshakable faith in God. And the insight that results from suffering gives me compassion for others. I listen to the still, small voice within. It has never led me wrong.

I once read that when Abraham Lincoln pondered a problem, he relied on God to talk to him. Lincoln was purported to have said, "I fell on my knees many times, simply because there was nowhere else to go." God led him to do what was right, bringing freedom to so many people. My hope is that these words will encourage you to fall to your knees and will also bring freedom to your heart.

Let's take comfort in the Sustainer of us all. Discover anew, beneath the sometimes tumultuous surface of life, the unchanging assurance of your Heavenly Father. His omnipresence is with us; His stabilizing Word that says, "I am with you, even in you," and His unstoppable, triumphant faith that is so uplifting and inspiring we find ourselves continuously walking in victory.

I thank God for the wonderful opportunity to know Him. Finally and above all, anchor your heart onto the promises of God and you will find, as I have found, so many, many times "God is with us."

Divine Love Yields Peace and Harmony

One of the most powerful lessons we have all come here on earth to learn is how to acquire pure and unconditional love. For one human being to love another, as God loves, is perhaps the most difficult of all tasks.

The relationship between a caring parent and child is the most heavenly form of human love that God has given to us. Perfect love is selfless; it loves without thought or reward. Those who live in tune with the power of divine love long to achieve harmony with their fellow human beings and peace with their nature.

How do you love when people have hurt you or rejected you?

You only need to ask yourself one question: What would Jesus do? That's because all those things happened to Him, through His enemies and His disciples.

Why did He allow it and continue to press toward the cross? Why do we suffer?

We suffer for others, as He did, so that they may come to know Him and have eternal life. God's Word shows us the example of perfect love in Matthew 5:44: "But I say unto you, love your enemies, bless them that curse you, do good to them that hate you, and pray for them which despitefully use you, and persecute you."

Are you carrying anger toward people who hurt you long ago? And the hurting source may still continue because weak people, motivated by evil gossip and designs, create cliques; they need to build each other up.

Do you want to be free of that? Do you want to forget it? I hope so, for to forgive and forget is to lift off the weight that stunts your own growth.

Whatever our sorrows may be, we must now put them aside so we will be able to live full, happy, and healthy lives.

Being embittered toward others ruins your joy. Some people carry bitterness with them for years and years. How many more of your precious hours will you worry yourself sick about a situation that happened weeks, months, or years ago?

The enemy wants you to feel sorry for yourself and keep you from loving and serving God. You belong to a heavenly realm. Don't waste any more time; let the hardness in your heart soften and say, "Enough is enough. I am going to forget it and put it in God's hands and leave it there."

Instead of being concerned about how others have hurt you and dwelling on the wrongs they have done, try thinking of a way to bring happiness to someone.

God loves you so much that He won't allow you to drown in self-pity if you call on Him. He wants you to have freedom from the enemy's relentless badgering. I know He said, "I came so you may have life and have it more abundantly, plus eternal life," and wrongdoing keeps you from that. When you have gone as far as you can go, do your best to love, and let God do the rest. I recall Him saying, "Don't be weary in well doing for you will reap when it's time if you faint not."

God provides us with many opportunities if we are alert enough to see them. Someone who needs encouragement may walk across your path. Minister to a neighbor; be kind to a coworker or boss. Don't miss the chance to give a token gift, praise their latest effort, and give them a sincere compliment.

Be thankful for the great gift of life. God gives a bushel of blessings for every ounce of praise. Center yourself on the Giver of life and feel the warmth of His love. For I read in John 15:5, "I am the vine: you are the branches. If a man remains in me and I in him, he will bear much fruit; apart from me you can do nothing."

It is so happy to love. There is no joy like His glory resting on you, and the glory of God is great!

The Storms We Face Make Us Stronger

For every hill you climb, each storm you face, and each disappointment you encounter, I like to remember what Joseph said in the Bible: "God meant it for good."

These obstacles are the experiences that make you strong. For the tears and heartaches, pain and anguish, difficult days and seemingly fruitless years . . . be thankful, because these are the things that make you great. The adversity and strife, the sweat and persistence are the stuff of which heroes are made.

History is full of those who have left their mark on the world because of the paths they have chosen to cut through. History tells us gold was purified by being beaten. When the purifier could see his reflection in the gold, it was perfect. And silver also was tried in the fire. The Bible says, "After you have suffered for a while you will be established, strengthened and settled."

You have only one life. It is your choice to become the beautiful creation God meant you to become or waste this process in sulking bitterness, mean retaliation, or futile ignoring of God. God never forces His character on anyone; you must humbly reach out and take this triumph and find in Him that which is altogether wise and strong and beautiful.

The Lord is our leaning post, our shelter. In His care we receive comfort and peace.

He can calm troubled waters when you walk out on them in faith. When you despair, He is there. When you feel helpless, know that the Creator of the universe is there for you. As you delight yourself in the knowledge of Him, He will give you the desire of your heart, and the joy of that knowledge will be your strength.

Depression is the design of the enemy to get you to look down, not up. The enemy thinks he is so mighty. Just wait and see how the mighty are fallen. Soon, one day, you will look and find that they won't even exist. They will be uprooted and be no more.

Pull your mind away from the negative conditions. Say to yourself, "I'm not going to let the enemy win." Then determine to do whatever it takes, and get up and over that obstacle. Do the first good thing that comes to your mind.

Trust God. Thank Him for what you do have, because the Word says, "In everything give thanks, for this is the will of the Father concerning you." Why does this help? Because it clears and opens the spiritual channels that God needs to pour out the hidden blessings in every experience He allows to happen in your life.

You are so secure and totally safe in the Lord's care. Pray and put the difficult situation in God's wise hands. He will honor that. When you stand for Him, He'll stand for you, so do not worry.

Two years ago a friend told me about her God box. If there is anything you need to talk to God about, you sit down and write God a letter, then put it in your God box. Your burdens will be lifted as you go your way in faith knowing that He sees the exact way to hurdle the obstacle or go through it to victory. A wise person turns great troubles into little ones and little ones into none at all.

The next time you encounter a difficulty or problem, use wisdom and say, "Here's my opportunity to grow." You can turn adversity into profit by gleaning every bit of character out of every obstacle.

Come let us join hands, leap over these obstacles, and be determined to praise God, for with Him we are victorious.

We See God in the Beauty All Around Us

It is only with the heart that a person can see rightly. What is essential and what matters most is invisible to the eye.

There was once a little boy who said to his mother, "Mommy, I want to see God." The mother answered, "No one can see God." So he decided to ask his Sunday school teacher. She also said, "No one can see God." Then he went to the pastor, and the pastor said, "God is a spirit . . . and no one can see Him."

One glorious summer day, the young boy went fishing with his grandfather. "Grandpa," he said, "can you see God?" The elderly man's eyes shone with a glorious light, and a beautiful smile came across his mouth. "Yes, I can see God." The little boy looked at him with awe and wonder. "Where, where is He," he shouted. The grandfather gently took his grandson in his arms and looked closely at his innocent face. "I am looking at God now . . . I see Him in the blue water of this pond, I see Him in the tree blossoms, and most important, my precious child, I see Him in you."

At this very special moment, refocus your vision, adjust your sight to see the world through such eyes. And miraculously, almost instantly, your life will change. "Open my eyes so that I may behold wondrous things."—Psalm 119:18.

Let God be in your heart and in your thinking. Let Him be in your mouth and in your speaking, in your eyes and in your looking. Recognize in others, in nature, and in your heart the radiance of God's own face.

Look on all things with love. Learn the art of seeing with the same mercy, compassion, and generosity as God does and you will rejoice in

His beautiful creation. There is no one so blind as he who refuses to see the opportunity to help another.

Treat others as you would like to be treated. We need one another. Be kinder than you have to be, more understanding and charitable. Say something nice to someone each day. It will give them a lift and you will get one also, from just being nice. The little things are so very important in life.

Give those who you meet a smile, a kind word, or a hand to hold. Shower loved ones with attention and affection. Soon, you will also be able to see God. He is hidden in life's little treasures: a tiny hand slipped trustingly in yours, a bouquet of flowers from your spouse, or a smile of appreciation from a neighbor.

Whenever you use the phrase "I see" in listening to a friend or loved one, you really mean you understand what they are saying. Your spirit has reached into the realm of their spirit with compassion and empathy. Such sharing is like a prayer being answered.

Keep your eyes on the Master. I recall the Bible says, "When we see Him we shall be like Him, for we shall see Him as He is."

Saturate yourself in God's loveliness. Everything He made is so sweet and precious. Take a walk outside, smell the freshly cut grass, feel the warmth of the sun on your face, look at the gorgeous flowers, and listen to the sounds of the ocean waves. Everything speaks of Him . . . all you have to do is look and listen.

To know Him is to obey His Word, and you will find that He is transforming love. Get up close, behold Him, and be changed into "A New You."

Take a Stand for Honesty and Integrity

*I*f you don't take a stand for what's right, you'll fall for anything. You only have one life; make it one of supreme moral courage. Live so you have no regrets.

A great example of integrity comes from a story about young Theodore Roosevelt. In his early years as a rancher out west, Roosevelt and some of his ranch hands were rounding up stray cattle. They wandered onto a neighbor's property, where they found an unbranded calf.

By the western tradition the calf belonged to the neighbor. One of Roosevelt's cowboys started to tie up the calf and put the Roosevelt brand on it. Roosevelt asked, "Why are you doing that?" And the worker replied, "It's gonna be your calf, boss." Incensed, Roosevelt said to the man immediately, "You're fired. A man who will steal for me will steal from me." Doing wrong never comes out right.

I love the saying, "Only one life to offer, it will soon be past, only what is done for Christ will last." Many great men and women have confessed that their greatest achievement was due to the power of God's Word brought forth in their life. That power gives persistence, perseverance, and success.

I know the Bible says, "What does it profit a man if he gains the whole world and loses his own soul?" How you live today will affect the peace in your life tomorrow. So make the right decisions now.

Everyone can start fresh with God. Each day is a new beginning. "The time is always right to do what is right," said Martin Luther King Jr. I recall the Word says, "Forgetting those things which are behind, press on to the mark of a high calling." Old habits die hard, but if God says forget, then forget.

I have a friend who told me that once her eyes were opened to the truths written in the Bible, from that day forward, she had to take a stand for them or for the rest of her life know she would be living a lie. How can you live with yourself when you compromise? What true success is there if something is gotten dishonestly? "Truth stands the test of time: lies are soon exposed."—Proverbs 12:19.

I find great joy in the knowledge that the Lord is always available to me. He fills me with a sense of quiet contentment that balances out the frustrations and despair that seem to pervade modern life and affect us all at one time or another. Sleep is sweeter for those who toil honestly, leaving their souls in God's care.

"Honesty is the first chapter in the book of wisdom," said Thomas Jefferson. Many highly successful people live by a code of super-honesty. They are not satisfied with just casual standards; they go the extra mile and make the right choices. Speak out against dishonesty, stand up for what is truth, keep your heart on target, and adhere to straight moral values.

Make today the day of decision. From this moment forward, walk through every minute of your life taking a stand for what is right.

Remember the knights in ages past? They were the noble ones riding out to crusade for what is right and to fight for what is right.

This is a new day. Ask God to forgive the past; determine in your heart to be true and noble from now on no matter what the cost. Knowing that you have taken a stand for that which is right with all your heart is such a great triumph for any life. You will have lived to the fullest, will have achieved the very best, and will have lived a life worthy of respect and honor.

Go Outdoors to Experience Nature's Grace

I love nature. All of the splendor and wonder around us is a loving expression of God. His divine beauty of character is revealed through the myriad forms of life He has created. Our reaction to the world that He so joyfully made affects our health and inner beauty. Stop for a moment to look at the sky, the flowers, and the trees; feel the atmosphere of God's love as He expresses Himself in this living masterpiece.

Man and nature; unseen angels and heavenly messengers; two different dimensions living side by side and intertwined. Isn't God amazing? Look what He put before us to see, feel, smell, taste, and hear. God put nature around us for a reason. It is healing, inspiring, and energizing. We need to get ourselves in touch and in tune with the symphony of creation so we can be all that He meant us to be and stay in our right minds.

Life can become so intense and stressful. Soothe your spirit and take relief from nature. Step into that almost heavenly dimension and you will begin to become a whole new person. Let the shores of peace lap healing waves over your mind, and find contentment and in the simple joys of life. Witnessing these innocent pleasures is like looking at God.

Watch in wonder how nature continually renews and refreshes itself and how serenely it accepts the changing seasons from summer to winter. Go outdoors, hike at one of our state parks, take long walks by the shoreline, or pick wildflowers along a country road. There are places to pick berries. Hunker down next to the warm, soft earth. The scent of berries in the air and the sweetness of the one you just popped into your mouth while listening to the birds sing can make you feel like a six-year-old again. It's good for the soul!

Hidden in the seemingly common and simple expression of nature is something mysterious and glorious. Reservoirs of wisdom and many of life's lessons are found here, inviting us to look beyond the ordinary and sense the presence of God. Through nature, God shows us what He wants us to be.

The trees are standing straight and tall, arms outstretched, praising God. Once in a while, you see a weeping willow, beautiful in its place, showing us that there may be sorrow in our life. But how many weeping willows do you see in comparison to all the other sturdy and uplifting trees? Not many.

Be patient in times of trouble, for I know that the Bible says, "By sorrow the heart is made better." As the glorious flowers open up to the sun, we must open to God and learn the secrets of His creation. Yield yourself to the thought, "What can this be showing me?" and allow the precious wisdom into your life.

"What do you think it means?" a friend asked as we both gazed in awe at the two tiny newborn baby birds peeking out from the freshly made nest cradled in her front door wreath. God is always speaking to us in nature . . . the love inside my friend's home even reaches beyond its doors.

During the storms the father bird watches carefully as the mother bird covers the babies with her wings. Soon morning comes, and the sun shines brilliantly through the crystal clear and freshly cleansed atmosphere. The mama bird returns to her nest with the food she gathered for her babies. How tenderly God teaches us, through the birds, not to worry about our life, or about what we will eat or drink, or what we will wear.

Look at the birds living in such joyful simplicity, taking wing and soaring above earthly cares, singing their praises to God. If a little girl watched the robins taking care of their nest and babies, she would learn, if she had no other example, how to take care of her own.

Nature is nourishment for our souls, peace for our minds, and assurance for our hearts, created by God, who I know said, "I will supply all of your needs [physically and psychologically] according to my riches and glory."

He's on Your Side Always and Everywhere

As a child, were you the one who was picked last for school sports teams, the one who was made fun of in high school, who was always in the last row in your dance recital, choir, or just did not fit in?

Were you ridiculed and looked down upon? Did the so-called "in crowd" reject you? Cliques among schoolmates, coworkers, or relatives hurt.

It can be devastating until you really begin to know God and His ways. He is fair to all. In the family of God you are accepted with warm, welcoming, open arms. He chose you first . . . even above Himself when He paid for all your sins. He chooses you to be on His team.

So do not be discouraged, even when those who are evil seem to succeed. See them for what they really stand for and know that you cannot join them wholeheartedly because your ways are far above them. Don't let bitterness build up; let go of any anger or resentment. It can fester up inside of you and do you great harm. Forget the mistakes of the past and press on to the greater achievements of the future.

Do not let anyone rob you of your joy and deter you from your goal. Get the burden off of your heart by telling God, thanking and continuing to praise Him. He will make a way for you to live far above those things. Find great comfort in knowing that even in your darkest hour, God is with you, promising never to forsake His own.

It doesn't matter to God what kind of house you live in, how popular you are, or how educated. But He does want to know . . . Do you love Him? He does want you to be like Him, joyful and invincible. If you have decided to love and serve God, I like to remember that He said, "You have not chosen me, I have chosen you." Let His arms hold you up and let Him get close to you. Try to treat everyone fairly, doing unto them as you would like them to do unto you.

Great men make you feel like the important one. Never get conceited in the blessings He gives you. A secret of real strength and power is to be humble. Remember the saying, "The way up is down." That's why those who reject Him rejected you. If you walk in His ways, consider such rejection the highest compliment. It is proof that you are not like the shallow, grasping masses.

I once heard a true story about a young mechanic who became a Christian. His coworkers and old crowd tested and teased him unmercifully. They called him an "oddball," "a fanatic," and "a nut." Day after day, they would scoff and say, "You are nuts." Suddenly, inspiration hit the mechanic and he turned to one and said, "This world is like a fine automobile. You take all the nuts out of it and what do you have? A bunch of junk!"

I thank God for these precious "nuts" whose prayers go up daily to Him. These are the prayers that hold this world back from destruction.

If you find that you don't go along with the crowd and that you are different, know that you are different for a reason. And that reason is because you are so very special to God and He has something special for you to do. It is His will for your life. As you seek Him, God will choose you to be lifted up into His presence, to be a representative of the King of Kings. You are the shining light, crowned with His love, the true treasure of His kingdom.

It is an honor to be different.

Pray and Pray Again, As Long As It Takes

I was having a particularly stressful day, when everything was magnified and needing to be done at once. It seemed to overwhelm me.

As I glanced down at the kitchen counter at the stack of mail yet to be opened, the little blue pamphlet stared back at me. I could almost hear the words speak to me that I read on the page. In bold letters it said, "Pray your way through."

Well, that was just the reminder I needed. Whatever the difficulty or dilemma may be, prayer brings forth peace. Many a time, when I pray through a problem, I find that the burden is totally lifted. Soon I feel rested and strengthened again. Prayer is one of the most important things in life to do.

We must be determined to pray until we have prayed through. This means that once we have finished praying, we know we have the answer.

"If we know that He hears us whatsoever we ask we know we have the petition that we desired of Him."—1 John 5:15.

You absolutely know the work is done. Pray until you are completely satisfied. Unless you are, you haven't prayed your way through.

It is so difficult to find the time to pray. It is such a battle to do the most important thing in life. We must become determined to make the time. Take the phone off the hook if you have to, turn off the television, and retreat to a quiet place where you can simply talk to God. Sometimes this seems almost impossible, but that just proves how valuable praying is.

Pray with all the fervor of your heart. Light up your soul with glory as you come into His presence. He will pour the liquid gold of His spirit like anointing oil over your bowed head and soothe your anxious soul.

I know that Scripture tells us, "And you shall seek Me, and find Me when you search for Me with all your heart."—Jeremiah 29:13.

Pull out all stops, bare your heart to God, ask forgiveness for any wrongs, and then know that He hears and answers prayers.

One of the greatest gifts we have is to really be able to pray for others, to intercede for someone in need. Prayers are the beginning of strength for the overcomer. Remember, if you are going to believe the Bible, you have to believe it all. It's not like a buffet dinner where you take some of this, but not that. God told Daniel, "Eat the whole roll."

There is a verse in the Bible I read that says, "These signs follow them that believe they shall lay their hands on the sick and they shall recover."

Agree in prayer that God will keep His word, and with faith watch miracles happen. What great character has the patient, persistent one who prays.

Sometimes, I feel that God's answer to the prayer of many a reader who asks Him to bless my weekly column is what gives me the inspiration to write. Prayers are powerful; do not underestimate yourself.

With God lies the answer to every desire you have in your heart. He will grant you all that you ask of Him according to His will. He always hears our prayers, whether He answers "Yes" or "Wait."

I know He said, "All things work together for good to those who love God and are called according to His purpose."

So put your worries, cares, or needs into His hands. He is faithful who promised. Wait in peace, wait in patience, sow in tears, reap in great joy, and praise Him who loves you so.

Confront Fears and Conquer Them

Remember the funny, floppy scarecrows, adorned with a big straw hat, plaid shirt, and old jeans, that the farmers used to put in their gardens before they started planting their crops?

As the wind would blow, the arms would move, and, it was hoped, the crow's would fly away.

One day a little chipmunk got into the farmer's garden and started eating the newly planted peas. Suddenly, a breeze came and the scarecrow's arms flapped in the wind. The chipmunk stopped and ran back a foot or two.

The animal looked around, studying the situation. When all was quiet and still, he began eating the peas again. And once more, with a puff of air, the scarecrow's arm shifted, while the chipmunk stood motionless. This time the animal didn't run away; he surveyed the area, and when nothing more happened, he just went right on around the scarecrow and had himself a feast!

There is much wisdom to be learned from nature. How many times have you started to break free from out of a rut and then something or someone shook you up and stopped you? Get past the fear . . . that is the secret. For the best things in life are behind the scarecrow!

To gain the good things in life and the greatest achievements, you sometimes have to go through difficult times. Dare to be all that you can be. Get to the feast of life and don't let obstacles get in your way. Do not be afraid or intimidated by the scarecrows—just realize that all they are is a puff of air, and go on past them to success.

To fight fear, confront what you are afraid of. "Do the things you fear and the death of fear is certain," said Ralph Waldo Emerson. Ninety percent of the things we fear will never happen. And for those circumstances that do occur, you can handle them all by being tough-minded.

Fill your mind with faith, for faith is stronger than fear. I know Psalm 34:4 says, "I sought the Lord and He heard me, and delivered me from all of my fears." Where there is doubt, replace it with hope. Expect the best, and most often positive results will follow, because you will get what you expect.

Do not be frightened. Get behind the fear, the insecurities, and the worries. There is an unseen enemy who wants you to doubt your God-given talents or intuition. But in that ability is the path to your greatest success. Be courageous. "Courage is the resistance to fear, the mastery of fear—not absence of fear," said Mark Twain.

A few weeks ago we put a bird feeder in our backyard. The blue jays, little sparrows, and lovely cardinals came to feed on the seeds and grain. There were also two beautiful mourning doves that flew down to the feeder. And then, with a great flurry, came six large, black crows . . . with their raucous caws. We observed that when the crows came, most of the small birds flew away immediately. But the sweet, gentle gray doves stayed, unafraid, and continued eating. The doves were not intimidated by the big, loud crows. They just continued on enjoying their feast and totally ignored the big, menacing birds. Almost instantly, the crows then flapped their wings and left.

We stood amazed at the lesson we had just seen. When you find something good in life, don't let anything hinder you. Behind those scarecrows is a feast of a new way of life.

So let the dove of peace rule your heart. Focus on the goodness in life, your goals and glorious dreams for the future. We've been made more than conquerors through Him who loves us.

With Faith, You Are Never Alone

"I will do better for you than at your beginning." I heard the Lord repeat in my mind those words that I read months ago. At that precise moment, at 4 A.M., I looked down at my sleeping baby's precious face and as I rocked her in my arms, I smiled up to Him and replied, "Lord, you already did."

When nervousness, frustrations, and difficult times come your way, I remember the Lord said, "Here I am . . . " Trust in Him who will not leave you. "Then shalt thou call, and the Lord shall answer; thou shalt cry and He shall say, Here I am."—Isaiah 58:9.

We all feel alone from time to time, when the cares of the world overwhelm us. If such feelings come to you, remember that Someone cares for you deeply, and do as I do, for the Bible says in Proverbs 3:5, 6: "Trust in the Lord with all your heart and lean not to your own understanding. In all ways acknowledge Him and He will direct your path."

He became a man and has walked this way before. Follow His footsteps and He will lead you out of the dark jungle of gloomy depression into the glorious sunlit meadow of His love. The way He lived and thought is the only way to true happiness. I read in God's Word, "Thy God hath anointed thee with the oil of gladness above all thy fellows."—Psalm 45:7. Follow Him.

Let your heart be patient toward God and watch Him work miracles in your life. He is right there waiting for you to follow Him so He can prove Himself to you. As you talk to Him, you will be aware of His strength-giving presence. Draw close to God and He will be very near to you.

Cast all your cares upon Him. Your Heavenly Father doesn't want you to worry. Give your concerns and woes into His mighty hands. Live on the joy of His promised word. Step on up higher to a life of faith and expectation. Be patient. God seldom does things instantly. Though He can perform instantaneous miracles, He usually takes His time to work things out.

"Why?" one may ask. "Why does He take so long?" I believe it's because in the time of waiting in faith, our true character is born. Your objective, attitude, and motive will determine the outcome of everything in your life. Wait in faith for His perfect solution. "If you have faith . . . nothing shall be impossible unto you."—Matthew 17:20.

Victory over any situation can be achieved by following God's advice. It's written for all to read in the Bible. You can overcome all things by the Word of God. Drop doubt from your mind. Believe that God wants the best for you and it shall happen. I know the Bible says, "According to your faith, be it unto you." So don't be discouraged. Give Him first place in your thoughts and in your plans in the morning and at night. And in the meantime, as Joshua 1:8 says, "Meditate on His word day and night that you may do all that is written there in. And you will make your way prosperous and you will have good success."

God will heap on you blessings upon blessings.

All day long as I work, my heart jumps with sudden joy as I pull my thoughts off the stress of business and turn to Him for a moment. Just as a long-distance runner pulls out a power drink and gulps it down—cool, refreshing, energy-giving liquid—so I pull my thoughts around to Him, and His smiling face pours into me refreshing strength and joy.

That's because I can see in His eyes that I am in this race to the end and I will receive the victor's crown and the trophy of my soul . . . His glorious character in me.

Be Positive and You Will Achieve Goals

"I have held many things in my hands and I have lost them all; but whatever I have placed in God's hands, that I still possess." — Martin Luther.

I agree with philanthropist George Muller that life has its share of hardships, losses, and disappointments, but I am not in the least tired, because I knew things would not always be easy. For the glory of God and the encouragement of His dear children, I desired to pass through these experiences one by one, if only others might benefit by the experiences I have encountered.

The hard times endured keep me sensitive to other people's troubles and sorrows. You cannot teach what you do not know.

The longer we live, the more trials of one kind or another we will have to overcome. But at the same time, we can grow happier and more assured that we are in the hand of God. Therefore, how can we grow tired of carrying on His work? God has proven many a time that He is faithful to His promises.

You have nothing to fear. Place your life, your family, career, and future in God's care. He will never steer you wrong. Have trust, as a small child believes in his or her parent, and rest in God who holds you safely in His hands.

Don't anticipate bad things happening. Immediately cancel out any discouraging thought that comes to mind. When you think or talk in a negative manner, then you can actually make that situation happen. Whatsoever you say will come to pass, so start now by saying aloud phrases like "Everything will be all right," or "I will do the best I can."

Make yourself a well of pleasant thoughts. Faithful sayings, inspirational reading material, and words of wisdom can carry you through trying times. A person is what he or she thinks about. So think and act hopefully and positively about everything, and expect great results.

You do not have to carry your burdens alone. I read in Psalm 46:1, "God is our refuge and strength, a very present help in times of trouble." Another way to get your mind off of your worries is to help someone else with theirs.

A Chinese proverb says, "When I dig another out of trouble, the hole from which I lift him is the place where I bury my own." Tell someone how much you appreciate them, give them a smile and encouragement. When we reach out to others, God sees the heart. When you are busy helping another, you won't have time to think about any problems of your own. And you will find you will be a happier person in the process.

Having a friend you can talk to and confide in is a great blessing. Everyone needs a comforter in a dark valley. There is no need to be lonely or to walk in darkness, because God Himself is the greatest comforter. No trial ever needs to be experienced alone; God has assigned a guardian angel to watch over us.

So with a heart full of faith, let us focus on all of the blessings and opportunities we have been given.

Day by day we will be renewed with the awareness of God's presence in our lives. He has great plans for you. I know the Lord said, "Behold . . . I have engraved thee upon the palms of my hands."—Isaiah 49:16.

Forget the Past and Soar onto a Higher Calling

An eagle flaps his wings once, and he's in the heavens. In one strong movement he is riding on the wind.

You, too, can be like the eagle by taking one verse of God: "Forgetting those things which are behind, press on toward the mark of the high calling in Christ."

According to the Old Testament, if you made a mistake or accidentally harmed someone, you could run to the temple and grab hold of the horns of the altar. Horns stand for power. I personally believe those two horns also represented the Old Testament and the New Testament. There you find grace and pardon.

Our past mistakes, the guilt and regrets, are sometimes overwhelming. In the journal of our lives we can restore the joy if we take hold of the Word of God and cling to it. Believing the Word brings forth power in your life. His infinite love can correct our thinking and make our paths straight. You want to walk in a certain way because you are transformed by believing His Word. So each day should be started with a prayer, thanksgiving, and reading at least one verse from the Bible.

I read in Joshua 1:3, 9, "I will give you every place where you set your foot. Be strong and of good courage. Do not be afraid, do not be discouraged, for the Lord your God will be with you where ever you go."

The Lord orders your footsteps, so you believe it and move forward. Place your foot on what God has promised and never doubt from this moment on that He is directing your path. God has plans for you. He will make a way when it seems like there is no way. Reach in your Bible and bring out a treasure, a jewel of the Word to share with others.

I know in Proverbs, it says, "The respect of God is the beginning of wisdom." Know that your past experiences have made you wise and caring. Many may benefit from this knowledge.

Don't let anyone intimidate you over past failures. The enemy knows your weak spot and tries to trip you up. Ask the Lord to give you the key so you can stand firm in your faith in God for your future and not be intimidated or resentful.

Take the shield of faith and the sword of the spirit, which is the Word of God. Jesus separates that which is truth from lies. When the sun rises in the sky, its light penetrates everything. Dark, creeping things scatter, and love breaks through. God is love, and that love expressed renders the devil helpless. How can the enemy hurt you when God is your defense and we are in heavenly places far above all principalities and powers? That enemy is under our feet.

Do not speak of past negative situations, especially with those you love. It will only hurt them. When people say hurtful things, hear their words with God's ears and wisdom. Let their darts stop with you. Take them to God in secret prayer. I read that the Bible says, "God hearing you in secret will reward you openly."

Then, forgetting those things that are behind, press on. "For if we walk in the light as He is the light then we have fellowship with one another and the blood of Jesus Christ cleanses us."

He will be the wonderful counselor and the prince of peace in your heart. You will rise up strengthened by His Word and know for certain that if God be for you . . . no man can prevail against you. You are always ultimately the winner.

So let us go on to receive the victor's crown.

Let God Provide the Foundation for Your Home

"We live by faith, not by sight."—2 Corinthians 5:7. I turned to the Lord for help in making a decision. "Build your house," He said. "All will fall into place. Your needs will be met."

So it began. With His blessing, the foundation of our heavenly dwelling was started. A home that will be filled with love, peace, and joy was being built bit by bit, line upon line, on solid rock. That rock is the Word of God.

"Therefore, who so ever heareth these sayings of mine and doeth them, I will liken him unto a wise man, which built his house upon a rock; And the rain descended and the floods came and the winds blew and beat upon that house and it fell not . . . For it was founded upon a rock."—Matthew 7:24, 25.

The storms of life that come against us will not threaten the stability of a house built on solid rock. The downpours, the drought, or the freeze will not weaken it. Your house must be built on wisdom so it will stand and not collapse. You, too, can have this wonderful revelation. You can change your world and create a home as it should be.

If you experienced a childhood in a house that was disturbing, you don't have to continue in that fashion. You have an opportunity to build or rebuild your own home.

We must create a home that has hidden strength. It's the dearest place to be. "Home is the definition of God," wrote Emily Dickinson. Our homes can be viewed as "heaven on earth"—a safe haven of stability, tranquility, and happiness. Even your decorations are an expression of yourself, your tastes, and love. The Lord wants you to have a happy home—a place filled with laughter, fun, and sharing, and with family, friends, and neighbors gathering together in kinship, building warm memories.

Let go of harsh noises and confusion and give soft answers. Do not quarrel or find fault with each other. Bring peace and harmony into your home.

Little droplets of kindness can smooth over any irritations of the day. A home is a place of give and take—a retreat, a place to rest and to enjoy life's simplest pleasures.

Our legacy of love is more valuable than all the money in the world, blessing our children with happiness. Base your home on these principles. Anyone can build a house, but only divine love makes it a home.

Our precious residence is an outward structure and example of our own eternal building. It was brought forth by sacrifice, faith, and love. Constructed by human hands but built by God.

His spirit dwells everywhere, from the colorful butterfly on the newly landscaped lawn to the honeybee buzzing in the clovers. While in the kitchen, I hear the sweet birds singing as they joyfully flock to their freshly made nests, and two blocks away, the church bells ring in perfect harmony.

In the dusk of the evening, the glistening stars are sitting prettily in the sky, as a backdrop to the chorus of crickets in the neighborhood. And as the day closes, I can almost see the wings of angels gathering around and protecting its frame.

As I walk though the threshold of our house, my heart is filled with praise to our Heavenly Father for helping me to find my way home. Never will I forget my Lord, who gave me this priceless gift . . . built on solid rock.

Include the Lord in your homemaking. Turn to Him, have faith, and your prayers for His perfect will shall be answered. He not only grants prayers, but He delivers even more and far greater than you can ever imagine. For in my Father's house are many mansions.

Don't Worry, God Provides Heavenly Help

A young mother had just fed her little baby son the last bit of food they had. There was nothing left; the cabinets were bare and the refrigerator was empty. After they finished eating, the gentle mother folded her hands over her son's hands and prayed, "Lord, there is no more food. It is up to You in Your mercy and love to care for us." With great faith, this dear mother knew God heard her prayer. She put the baby in his playpen and started cleaning the windows.

Thirty minutes later, the doorbell rang. There stood a sweet, smiling lady the young mother had never seen before. The lady said, "I'm newly attending your church and they told me you lived out my way. I thought we could have some fellowship." The young mother happily invited the lady in and they began to talk of the love of God.

After they visited for a while, the lady asked for a glass of water. Then baby started fussing, and the lady said, "Take care of the baby. I'll get the water."

The young mother told the lady there was cold water in the refrigerator, forgetting that there was nothing else. She heard the cabinet doors opening and shutting and called out, "The glasses are at the right-hand side of the sink."

A few minutes passed and the lady said she had to go and pick up her four daughters from school, but said she would return with them because she wanted the young mother to meet her children.

An hour later, the doorbell rang again. When the young mother opened the door, there was the sweet lady with her four daughters, each holding a bag of groceries, five full bags of food. The sweet lady said, "I hope you don't mind. I saw the cabinets were bare."

Through teary eyes filled with joy, the young mother hugged the lady and her girls and said, "Thank you, Lord." That family had nothing left to eat, but in three hours they had everything . . . all from someone they had never seen before. This is a true story.

God will supply all of your needs. His promises never fail. Believe in the pure word of God. He's always on time. I know that the Bible says in Psalm 138:3, "On the day I called, you answered me, you increased my strength of soul." So trust in that great love and live to please Him.

When you have gone as far as you can go, that's when God steps in and performs miracles. Do not worry, fret not; God meets every desperate need. There is no fear in love. If you live long enough in the light of God's perfect love, you will not be afraid.

Saturate yourself in His Word. Shut out all the unbelievers. You just do not have time for their negativity. This is your life. It is valuable and can be glorious. Open yourself up to the truth, the way, and the life, and drink it like a desert wanderer takes water.

Like a flashlight in a dark room, shine God's light upon your heart. Take time to talk with Him often, and with prayer and thanksgiving make your requests known to Him. Then trust, trust, trust. He is a miracle-working God.

Fear not and believe only. Be shut in with the safety of God, who has thousands of angels to do His bidding, to put ideas in your head, and thoughts of kind deeds to do for others. God will give you the power to live in victory. His perfect love will cast out all fear. He is the only one who can do that, as He has done all down through history for so many.

Just take His promise, keep it close to your heart, and believe it.

Hold onto God's unchanging hand. He is the same yesterday, today, and forever.

Departed Loved Ones Are Never Very Far from Us

Looking down from the heavens, departed loved ones are always with us. The memories of their words, the warmth of their smile, and the love of their lives are alive in our hearts, providing comfort. They are just a thought away, and their wisdom can continue to give us strength for the challenges that lie ahead.

It was one of the last things a dear mother wrote in her journal before she died: "When God calls, I will let you know when I arrive on the other side. I will ask Him to send a storm on the day of the funeral."

Bright blue and sunshine filled the sky as family members and friends gathered to remember this mother so fondly. Not a cloud was to be found. The weather report called for clear and dry conditions for the next three days.

That afternoon, a luncheon was held in her memory, and by 5 P.M. most of the guests had gone home. As the family was clearing the dishes from the dining-room table, a loud rumble startled them. All at once, black clouds blanketed the sky and thousands of huge raindrops poured down in masses. Thunder and lightning filled them with solace, awe, and joy as they found hope in the storm.

It's been said that death is far from being the end, but an open door to an existence larger, brighter, and more blessed than this.

Even though our loved ones can look over the banisters of heaven, they can never feel sorrow over our trials, for they know, as the Lord does, that all things work together for good for those who love God and are called according to His purpose.

His ultimate design for us is to have His love and to live with Him eternally. Upon leaving this world, there is a world of endless sunshine, for we are children of the light. People who have experienced the light of great love at the end of a tunnel, before being brought back to earth, have written about it in many books. We have been given these various examples so that we know they are not coincidences.

I have a friend whose Christian mentor died suddenly of a heart attack. Shocked and in grief, she jumped into her car and drove an hour and a half to get to her friend's house to comfort her children. As she was driving and crying, she was aware that another presence came into the car, one of great love and joy. She knew that it was the spirit of her friend, and she felt her friend saying, "Oh, I am so happy, so free and full of God. I'll see you again and we will be together with Jesus in eternity."

This experience repeated itself three times before she got to her destination. What a comfort it was when she told her friend's children. It was like the women who went to Jesus' tomb and came running back to the disciples saying, "He is risen, He is risen."

So, dear readers, I want to pass along to you the joy I feel when I look up to the stars at night and think, "My mother, great in her faith and thankfulness for the joys of life, must surely be in their midst." Sometimes, when the clouds part, I think of the light of her radiant smile and I know she still watches over me. And I know that the angels, ministering to us, are carrying out the wishes of the Almighty.

True Love Lasts Through Time

Love at first sight is easy to understand. It is when two people have looked at each other with a revelation that this love is forever after years and years together . . . it is then that it becomes a miracle manifested.

True love is eternal. Not time nor age nor circumstance can diminish genuine and pure love. I recall that the Bible says, "Many waters cannot quench love, nor floods drown it." Waters of multitudes of people, waters of trials and disappointments, or floods of financial difficulty—true love goes beyond ecstatic emotions. True love is a commitment. That is why it lasts after the honeymoon is over. It lasts for richer or poorer, in sickness or in health. It is the daily triumph of integrity over skepticism.

Love grows when it is watered daily with kind words and deeds. "Where do you call home?" a man asked another traveler while on a business trip. The traveler answered, "Wherever she is," as he smiled and pointed to his wife.

Do you know that women set the mood of the home? Decorate your home not only with beautiful flowers and lovely pictures, but also with a gentle and positive spirit, looking lovely and fresh each day, as true loveliness comes from a sincere appreciation between husband and wife.

The more you complement your spouse and genuinely say, "Honey, you're the best husband in the world," or "You're a wonderful wife, darling," the more they'll become what you have spoken. Speak what you see possible within them.

Words are powerful. They can transform. Each evening, comment on something he or she did that day that you enjoyed or that made you happy. Give thanks for each other. We are little creators, made in God's own image, so it is possible to do impossible things with His help.

Marriage and family therapists say the small, daily acts of kindness make the biggest impact on your relationship. Those tender tiny acorns of love can grow into mighty oaks shading and sheltering your hearts and homes.

Leave love notes on his or her pillow. Send a card to let them know they are in your thoughts. Share joyous laughter. Smile. If you look happy, it will eventually become a fact. Vow to let the little annoyances pass.

Don't take each other for granted. Compliment your mate in front of family and friends. Reminisce about wonderful memories. A friend of mine told me a cute story. On Saturday nights, after she and her husband put their three young daughters to sleep, they sometimes order take-out and pretend they are dining at a restaurant.

Bake his favorite dessert, something that will make the house smell yummy! Eat dinner by candlelight; it will give him something that makes a long, hard day's work worthwhile.

Bring home flowers for her for no reason. Studies confirm that the first five minutes you spend together at the end of the workday will set the tone for the evening, so put aside the nagging problems for a few hours, a few days, or even forever.

Show your love and appreciation by all that you do, say, think, and pray. You have heard the old saying that "The family that prays together stays together." It is absolutely the truth. To sit together and hold each other's hands to talk with your Heavenly Father is the cornerstone to building a deep and lasting marriage. Don't underestimate the power of prayer. If you are really serious about a "marriage made in heaven," this is the only way.

To have true love is somewhat like building a fine character. It is not a gift, but a victory, day by day, year by year . . . eternally!

Please, Dear Lord, Help Me to Be Like Mom

I dedicate these words to my mother and to beloved mothers everywhere. It is a time of reflection and thanksgiving.

My heart stirs as I search my mind to remember . . . It seems hard to believe that fifteen years have come and gone since my mother passed away.

I recall her saying to me, "If I could only go back in time and know then what I know now." I try to recollect bits and pieces of her wisdom. But, if I only knew then what I know now . . . How I long today for my mother's gentle touch, keen observations, and loving advice.

It never occurred to me, even once, that she would be gone in the blink of an eye. If that insight had been revealed to me, I would have savored every minute I had with her. I would have asked her a thousand questions and we would have shared so much more.

Mothers are the source from which we derive the guiding principles of life. It's been said, "The hand that rocks the cradle rules the world." George Washington wrote, "All I am, I owe to my mother. I attribute all my success in life to the moral, intellectual, and physical education I received from her." A mother's heart is the classroom of a child. That love endures beyond time and death.

My mother taught me to be kind. "Be nice and love everyone," she would say. I learned what it means to love unconditionally and to give up everything for your family.

When you have a child, you only want what makes them happy; you forget self.

My mother's truth and insight still rings in my ear, and the sweetness of the tone in her voice guides me onward. But God has also sent me substitute mothers—"angels," as I call them—who have helped me along the way and who give me strength and comfort.

If you haven't been blessed with a wonderful mother, ask God to lead you to someone who has a real mother's heart. He has someone out there for you.

My mother and I had an unspoken trust. On Mother's Day years ago, I placed a small box of chocolates with an "I love you" note attached under my mother's pillow. She loved it and thus it became a ritual—not just on Mother's Day, but at other times, too.

We'd pass under-the-pillow notes and gifts from my pillow to hers. As a little girl, I recall asking Mom not to show the notes to anyone . . . they were just for her and they'd be our little secret. So she never spoke of our under-the-pillow messages.

Not a day goes by that I do not think about my precious mother. Writing this for you, dear readers, makes me tremble with a longing to hug her and tell her that I love her. Through my tears, I think it's important for you, my friends, to learn from my experience. So right now, today, while you still can, write those notes of appreciation, say those words of love and thankfulness, and give your mother an extra-long hug!

The day after my mother passed away, I found the little bundle of notes, cards, and letters I gave to her through the years, tied with a faded pink ribbon and tucked under her mattress. Gently, I held the notes to my heart and whispered a prayer that has clung to me all my life. It was the greatest compliment I could say: "Lord, please, in all her good and kind ways, make me like my mother."

Have Faith, and All Things Are Possible

The strongest oak tree is not the one that is protected from the raging hail and violent winds or hidden from the sweltering heat. It is the one that endures the storms, bends in the wind, and struggles patiently to live in the heavy heat.

It has one objective in mind: "I am going to survive; I am going to stand tall after all."

Faith, faith, faith is the key that unlocks the door to dreams being fulfilled. There is no royal, easy highway to success—one step at a time and all things in succession. That which grows slowly, believing, will endure.

Success takes time. "Genius is nothing but a greater aptitude for patience," said Benjamin Franklin. Thomas Edison said, "If we did all the things we are capable of doing, we would astound ourselves."

Do you have a dream? Your heart's desire? A plan? Don't give up. You can win the race if you count on God and work toward your goal with all your heart. With God all things are possible. Look upon His face, see His head nodding reassuringly as each day you take one small step ahead. The good Lord's grace will be with you as you travel on through the valleys and over the mountains.

God answers prayer when you determine to give Him the glory. We are humbled in thanksgiving as we see His generosity and power to supply all our needs.

"Now to Him who is able to do immeasurably more than all we ask or imagine, according to His power that is at work within us, to Him be glory . . . "—Ephesians 3:20.

Never, ever think that you can succeed in life without Him. You may feel you may be doing pretty well on your own. But live long enough and you will experience the bitter taste of defeat if you have left God out of your life. It is your choice. Choose Him and all of life is sweet. Even the bitter is bittersweet. Choose life without Him and it's downhill all the way to loneliness, emptiness, and unhappiness.

If even one person is drawn to the Lord, then, as I read in the Bible, "there will be great rejoicing over that one soul in Heaven."

Prisoners say that in the confines of a penitentiary, the only freedom they had was the freedom to choose how to think. When they chose to think on the Lord Jesus Christ, He personally walked through stone walls and sat at the table in their hearts and became the complete joy of their lives.

God never changes. He is the same yesterday, today, and forever. And when they got out of prison, their paths were set on His directions to true joy and life everlasting. I like to remember that in His Word, He says in Jeremiah 29:11, "For I know the plans I have for you, plans to prosper you and not to harm you, plans to give you hope and a future."

The path the Lord has chosen for you will perfectly lead you to the plans He has for your life. Everything that happens is significant and is working together for good. You are never alone in your pursuits. There is a Heavenly Father who walks beside you to guide you. Practice listening to that still, small voice within. God knows perfectly where your path will lead. He predestined us to live for His glory. So do not worry about tomorrow; God is already there.

Many times we may falter and are overcome with despair. But we must trust God and have the determination to never give up.

There are incredible things that await you; all you have to do is have faith and joyful expectation, which is the outward manifestation of confident hope.

Fill your heart with hope and joy. He is God, and with God, all things are possible . . . only believe.

Do Good, Do Right, Despite All

Yes, it came at a time when I needed it the most. I was down, disheartened, and discouraged. How miraculously God works and supplies our greatest need with the most perfect timing.

A dear reader sent an article to me written by Mother Teresa. The words rang so true as I opened my mail at just the right moment. I couldn't control the tears as I read these words:

"People are often unreasonable, illogical and self-centered: forgive them anyway. If you are kind, people may accuse you of selfish, ulterior motives. Be kind anyway. If you are successful, you will win some false friends and some true enemies. Succeed anyway.

"If you are honest and frank, people may cheat you. Be honest and frank anyway. What you spend years building, someone could destroy overnight. Build anyway. If you find serenity and happiness, others may be jealous. Be happy anyway.

"The good you do today, people often forget tomorrow. Do good anyway. Give the world the best you have and it may never be enough. Give the world the best you've got anyway. You see, in the final analysis it is between you and God. It was never between you and them anyway."

In business, in school, and even in family life, these words are words of great wisdom. Maybe I will never understand the attitude of strife, jealousy, and envy. And you know what? I don't want to. It is wisdom to recognize that in this world evil does exist, but it doesn't have to change you. Heartaches are to be put in the Father's hands and left there.

Wrongful actions by some can leave you feeling numb, unable to sleep soundly, and burdened by stress. But let the sun go down upon your hurting heart knowing that the problem is not you. It is with them. Those hurtful people and their spiteful tactics will soon meet their end.

Give problems to the One who can give peace through it all. I find strength in you my Heavenly Father, who said, "Every weapon that is formed against you will not prosper." He will work things out for His good and your glory. This time of heartache will pass as you get closer to the One who loves you unconditionally, and your life will once again become serene in His care.

We are in a battle and are sometimes prisoners of war. What do prisoners of war do to survive? They use their mind to think on that which is good, lovely, and just, not on the conditions around them that they cannot immediately change. So to combat negativity, surround yourselves with loving friendships, gather goodness from life, and clothe yourself in joy and thanksgiving for what is good and right.

It is extremely important that we put aside all our daily concerns and make time for communion with God on a daily basis. Our souls need the peace and understanding we receive when we draw close to our Creator.

Expressing our thoughts to God and listening to His response brings wisdom, peace, and contentment. As we lean on Him, our cares and woes come into perspective and His love and joy become the greater object of our thoughts. I know He said, "Forgetting the things that are behind, press on the mark of the high calling (Christ in you)."

Press through the stress to His side. Press through the mess of busy life. Press through the spiteful actions of small-minded people. Press into the kingdom of God. Remember—the kingdom of God is within you. It is a place for all the weary, a place where you can find real peace, sitting at the table in your heart with Jesus, where all your cares and heartaches cease. There you gain the wisdom, strength, and courage to go on.

So press into the kingdom, dear readers . . . press on.

No Greater Power Than Our Love for Others

I once heard a very touching story about a girl who was suffering from a rare disease. Her only chance of recovery was to have a blood transfusion from her five-year-old brother. He had miraculously survived the same disease. The doctor explained the situation to her brother and asked the young boy if he would give his blood to his sister. The little fellow took a deep breath and said, "Yes . . . I will do it to save my sister."

As the transfusion began, the small boy, with tear-filled eyes and trembling voice, asked the doctor, "Will I die right away?"

That little boy thought he had to give his sister all of his blood.

I recall that the Bible says, "Greater love has no man than he that would lay down his life for a friend." There are three things that endure: faith, hope, and love . . . and the greatest of these is love. Children have a wondrous capacity to love. Because they come so fresh from heaven, saturated in the Father's love, that's all they know. Filled with God's character, they love unconditionally.

We should strive for this childlike love. Even for us as adults there is a way back to innocence, peace, and joy, no matter what we have done before. "And above all things, have fervent love for one another, for love will cover a multitude of sins."—1 Peter 4:8.

The grace of God's mercy is deep and powerful. It can transform you into "A New You."

Love is defined in the original Greek language of the New Testament as "agape," meaning God's fruit of love gives itself away purely and generously to express God's nature and divine compassion.

God is love, and what is so wonderful about His love is that it is transforming love. It can completely change us. I recall that the Bible says, "As we look to Him, as we look at a mirror, we are changed from glory to glory." Therefore God has the power to make all things new.

What a glorious world it would be if we could all just love one another.

Don't be like the little fish that was afraid to drink the water. The mama fish asked her small son, "Why won't you drink more water?" With a worried look the little fish said, "Mama, I'm afraid I may drink it all up."

Now, that may sound silly, but some people are frightened to reach out and take in all the gifts of God freely. God is a vast ocean of love, free to everyone. You can never outlove God.

Love is expressed by the tone of our voice, the words we choose, our actions, and most of all the motivating spirit behind them.

Do a kind deed for someone in secret. It may be a small treat on a coworker's desk, a card of good cheer, or even cutting a neighbor's lawn while they are not home. The more you give, the more, in turn, you will have. Laughter, a smile, a prayer, can bring such happiness to others.

The art of giving, without expecting compensation, is vital to abundant life. Studies reveal that those who volunteered at least once a week outlived those who did no volunteer work, by a ratio of two and a half to one. So helping others is a powerful contributor to health and well-being.

Love is always so gracious, so humbly sweet, and love is also powerful, the most powerful force on earth. "There is no fear in love, but perfect love casts out all fear."—1 John 4:18.

Love is so courageous. As that little boy so loved his big sister, we all have a Brother who loved us so much that He laid down His life so that we could live. Thousands who have chosen to believe it received the transfusion of that powerful love, and it is the greatest treasure we can take with us. Be strong in His love and rejoice in His love, for God is love.

Love of Money Is the Root of All Evil

A wonderfully wise and dear woman once said to me, "If you want to see the true character in a person, touch their wallet."

Once there were two friends walking across the road. "We've been good friends for a long time . . . ," said one friend to the other. "Yes, indeed, we have," was his reply.

"We could share anything with each other, right?"

"Sure we can," his friend agreed.

"If you had a million dollars, would you give me half?" the friend asked.

"Yes, I would," the other confidently stated.

"If you had two cars, would you give me one?"

"Yes, I would," he said.

"If you had half a million dollars, would you give me half?"

"Sure, I would."

Then the friend suggested slyly, "If you had forty dollars, would you give me half?"

The man looked irately at his now ex-friend and grumbled, "That's not fair . . . you know I have forty dollars!"

This is a funny little joke, but it shows me what the Bible says to be true: "The love of money is at the root of all evil."

For a few swiftly passing dollars, some people will lose friends and sell their own soul. Instant gratification can lead to eternal desperation. In the Word of God it asks, "Why do you spend your money for that which does not satisfy?" So many people think, "If I only had that (whatever), I would be happy," "If I only had that car, that job, that house, or that person I know, I would be happy and satisfied."

Then they begin to scheme to achieve their end. They cheat in business deals, lie, covet, and labor. They obtain their coveted desire and soon realize, after only a very short while, that they still feel empty and unhappy. Their gain has not satisfied them.

Those who possess God-like character only want to give and would rather share what they have than receive. Why? Because the Word of God is true and it says, "It is more blessed [happy] to give than to receive."

A reader wrote via e-mail, "I am a single mother of four beautiful children. Life has not been easy, and trying to give these kids the things they need has been a challenge, but with the help of friends, family, and strangers, I have made it through so much. Some people will never know how the smallest gift can help someone."

Albert Einstein said, "Comfort and happiness have never appeared to me as a goal." Living life to satisfy yourself is totally and utterly selfish. To give to others is the goal, and happiness is just the by-product. Remember the little butterfly of happiness? It always flits away when you chase it, but if you get busy doing something kind for someone, it comes and sits upon your shoulder.

By seeking to make others more comfortable, we find our beds the most comfortable at night and we sleep the unbroken sleep of the blessed. Happiness can never be bought with money. It is free to those who give of themselves to others, give of their time, empathy, and heart. Doing unto others as you would have them do unto you is to prove to yourself how deep is the wisdom of God.

How does this golden rule bring happiness into your lap? I do not know, but the Creator of the universe has made it a law as sure as the law of gravity. And I have found it true by personal experience.

Prayers Are the Sweetest Perfume

I read that somewhere in Europe, a certain type of rose must be plucked in the dark of the night in order to bring forth the greatest perfume within. How God loves it when we are awakened in the night and turn our thoughts and prayers to Him. The sweetest perfume to Him is our prayers.

When our children come to us with a difficult problem, it gives us such pleasure when we can solve it simply. It is the same joy our Heavenly Father feels when we put our cares and fears into His hands. Just lean on Him and watch how He makes them work together for good. What an honor it is to have such a wonderful parent as God. There is no better honor in the world.

God can do incredible things. The touch of the Master's hand can transform a life. He can give you all the strength needed to live in victory. I have found that the secret is to read His Word daily and strive to align my life with it, checking, checking, and double-checking my motive, objective, and attitude by it. Daily conversations with God bring everything into perspective.

We can only know the mind of God by reading His Word. Can any student pass a test in nuclear physics without knowing the subject? Or without taking time to study? Impossible. And so it is with passing the tests of life; we must know God and study His book even if it means burning the midnight oil.

A reader wrote, "The only way to get true peace in life is with a relationship with God. He wants you to spend time with Him. I bring every situation to the Lord. By relinquishing things to Him, I have peace."

King David, a mighty warrior whom God said was a man after His own heart, was sometimes afraid, as we all are. I know He wrote in Psalms, "What time I am afraid, I will trust in the Lord." To conquer fear, we must trust God and thereby triumph over every obstacle. We must keep our eyes on the promises of God. This alone will give us courage.

"The optimist sees opportunity in every danger, the pessimist sees danger in every opportunity," Winston Churchill said.

We all go through the dark nights, but if we yield ourselves to God, He will pluck the strings of our hearts, bring forth the music of our prayers and praise, and give us perfect peace because our minds are stayed on Him. Always believe that God will make a way where there is no way, and that if it is His will, your prayers will be answered.

Great contentment can be found in the power of prayer. It can restore, refresh, and give guidance for your problems while enabling you to master and overcome any situation. Through prayer, God speaks to you, too.

I am so comforted to know that God answers prayer and that He is in perfect control. He never sleeps or slumbers; the day and night are both alike to Him. The greatest force in the world is His love, and that love never fails.

There is no fear in love. Perfect love casts out all fear, and God's love for us is the only perfect love there is. Every moment of every night can work for our good. If we sleep, we are renewed in body. If we are awake and pray and praise, we are renewed and refreshed in our spirit. In the dark of the night, the prayers we send up to Him, through the twinkling stars, bring forth the sweetest perfume.

Your Inner Voice Will Guide the Way

I read in the Bible, "The kingdom of God is within you." God put within me a dream for my future. Sometimes, it seemed a distant dream on a path winding, rough, and narrow, with roadblocks and obstacles all along the way. Would God give me this dream, though, without helping to make it come true?

Through many miles of uphill climbs, rocky roads, and mountains that at times appeared to be unmovable, I asked, "Lord, have you forgotten me?" Suddenly, a peace washed over my heart and deep within a small, soft voice said, "I have not forgotten you . . . I have plans for you, plans to give you hope and a future."

Since then, I have listened closely to this inner resource and it has never steered me in the wrong direction. By the same quiet voice, my instincts and gut feelings have rescued me dozens of times. And when I listened and trusted those inner resources, favorable results always followed.

Your insight can help you to achieve your goals. Many a time, an individual's belief, strong vision, and inner knowledge were motivating factors that led them to success. Learn to listen closely to your inner self . . . Your destiny lies in the balance.

Deep within there is a vast reservoir of untapped power just waiting to be used. Utilize this resource to guide your life confidently in the right direction.

Remain open to ideas that come into your mind. As you spend quiet moments in solitude, great thoughts and creative ideas can flow freely.

In this busy world, take time to meditate at the start of the day; slow down and pray. When you pray, you have clear insight into your inner self, and the product of that is making you a better person.

The best inspiration often comes first thing in the morning, before any distractions of the day can come your way. Wake up an hour earlier. Let this be your time to focus clearly on your inner calling.

Live your life based on inner signals. Follow your inward leading. Sharpen your intuition, your inner voice and conscience. Be aware of its power and, though it speaks very softly, the answers will be quite clear.

Be careful of people who, with charming ability, undermine your beliefs. If you get an uneasy feeling around them, listen to that inner voice. If it says "clear out," then run away fast! Sometimes, when we want something very much, we ignore the warning signs. But your life is far too valuable to be used by someone or something that doesn't have your best interest at heart. That quiet, little nudge is your best friend.

Surround yourself with creative people. Be like the artists that congregated together in Paris. Their creativity fed each other and produced masterpieces for the world to admire.

Though the charted courses of life can be rough and rocky, with bends, turns, and detours, we must thank the Lord for having destined plans for our lives, and trust in Him to make our paths straight.

And as Ralph Waldo Emerson wrote, "What lies behind us and what lies before us are small matters compared to what lies within us."

Take a moment now, dear readers, in silence, to hear the whisper of that still, small voice. Close your eyes and listen . . . listen . . . listen . . . It is telling you that you are precious, and each day is a miracle.

Reassuring Words Smooth Life's Bumps

"Everything will be all right," "I know how you feel," "Don't worry," "Remember how God brought you through last year and the year before, difficulties you don't even think of anymore."

Comforting words of reassurance to warm, calm, and to let you know that this time of confusion will soon pass. These simple phrases, when spoken by a trusted friend or loved one, can console, strengthen, and get you through life's difficult moments.

Sometimes you feel you can't go on any longer. Hold on; give it a day or two. Soon, things will begin to get better. If you are experiencing periods of sadness and you don't know why, just wait. Look up, beyond the clouds, to the pure blue sky where the soaring birds wing. The good Lord spread above us a precious canopy of blue to remind us to have patience in times of trouble.

"They that wait upon the Lord shall renew their strength; they shall mount up with wings as eagles; they shall run and not be weary; and they shall walk and not faint."—Isaiah 40:31.

We go through many storms throughout our lives, but always remember that somewhere up ahead, the clouds will clear and the sky will once again be bright, and the sun will glisten down on the petals of the lily in the field.

Just as the flowers need rain to grow, sometimes we must bear sorrow for our lives to be enriched and bloom. If we but ask and believe, angels are always at our side to guide us through times of need, according to our Father's direction. Know that there is a heavenly host around you—a divine love that reveals itself through the little things, the simple everyday tasks if done as unto the Lord.

How comforting to know that we have a Father who loves us. That love is steadfast, constant, and consistent. We must have a steadfast, constant, and consistent awareness of the One who cares for us so. Just this awareness will create miracles.

Nature can teach us a multitude of things. We learn so much from all of nature, from the tiniest creature to the grandest oak. Watch in wonder as the cute and perky squirrels energetically gather nuts. Instinctively, they know to collect their food and store it up for when the hard times come. We all need to be like them and collect God's happy promises and store them in our hearts for when the difficulties arise.

Imitate the oak tree and lift up your arms and praise God. For God in His strength and love inhabits the praises of His people. Every member of God's creation is linked by a common thread. Outside the window I see two soft doves snuggling side by side on a branch. The comforting sweetness of the doves reveals to me the importance of being there for our fellow neighbors, friends, and loved ones, cooing happiness for their success, and when times are low, supporting them and raising them up with soft words of love.

If you feel overwhelmed, spend at least ten minutes talking to the Lord. Ask the questions, listen, and watch nature for the answers. "In all ways acknowledge Him and He will direct your path."—Proverbs 3:6.

God will direct your footsteps to great fulfillment and countless blessings. There is no sweeter joy than a relationship with Him. His love surpasses all other love. He will do for you what you cannot do for yourself.

Give every problem to Him. His constant reassurance is so warm and comforting. I meditate on His Word and hear His voice saying, "Let not your heart be troubled." He is as close as a heartbeat. Look around you and see His problem-solving wisdom in all of nature. And like the still waters of the lakes and pools, reflect the greatness of His love.

Children Learn How to Love from Parents

*I*nvisible to my eyes, my daughters have been observing their parents' actions and words. And now, I begin to see the manifestation of all they have heard and seen in their young, formative years.

For our daughter's third birthday, my husband and I casually asked her, "Sweetheart, what gift would you like for your birthday?" Sweetly, she responded with a smile, "I'd like a book, Mommy." Then, without even pausing for a breath, she added, "And I'd like a book for my sister, too!"

How precious this response was to me. And how it delights my heart and soul to know that she so quickly thought of sharing her gifts.

Ever since we bought a fish tank, our little girls have been diligent in making sure the fish are taken care of. Every night, before bedtime, the girls give the fish tank a great big hug and say, "I love you fis-s-hies, sleep tight." I believe animals are sensitive to our spirit. I'm sure those fish feel the love right through the glass.

The other evening, as we sat in the living room, we heard in the distance the sound of a fire engine's siren. Both our daughters, even the little one-and-a-half-year-old, immediately folded their hands in prayer. Our three-year-old said, "An emergency truck, Mommy . . . let's pray." And so we prayed for whoever it was who needed the fire truck. Then the children were satisfied that God would take care of it and happily turned back to their play.

One glorious afternoon, we were visiting a farm market. The man who runs the farm told us that one of the ponies on the farm had injured itself. My daughter looked up at me with wide eyes of compassion and said, "Let's bring that pony an apple next time we come here."

And I think I was asked the question of all questions. As my little one held out her scraped finger, she asked, "Mommy, why does God give boo-boos?" Wow . . . I knew I had to answer her with all the sincerity of my belief. "Well, my darling," I replied, after pausing a moment, "God doesn't give us hurts, but He sometimes allows them to happen because He knows that as we get over them, we are stronger and it gives us greater character."

Now, more than ever, parents need to be spiritual teachers. Children raised with spiritual understanding will know how to quiet their hearts and that God will watch over them. Let children know that God loves them very much and that they are here for a very special reason. As the children grow, they will know to listen to His voice as a guide to help them choose right over wrong.

Strength of character is acquired at home. There the affections are trained and the quality of love learned. Create an atmosphere of trust, love, and acceptance for the children, and bring forth these attributes early on.

An infant is like malleable gold. Cherish their innocence. Holding, cuddling, and singing to your baby will let them see the light of love in your eyes and will allow them to flourish and become a warm, giving, and loving person, just as a flower will grow and bloom in the light of the sun.

Let them know that they have special gifts within them that could change other people's lives and could encourage their dreams. Practice a period of silent time with your children, teaching them that five minutes or so of being alone and quiet can be very enriching. It can reveal the closeness of God.

Pray for God's guidance in raising your children, and trust in His Word. We always ask God for help, and each new day uncovers His wonderful love and sweetness in my tiny girls.

Open Your Eyes to the Blessings Around You

There once was a story about a man who looked up at the heavens and called out, "God, speak to me." And a mockingbird sang every praise possible, but the man did not pay attention to the glorious melody.

Again the man asked, "God, will You speak to me?" as the wind rustled through the trees and made the leaves clap their hands, but the man did not hear.

Looking from side to side and frowning, the man said, "God, I want to see You." An exquisite rose gave its fragrance out into the sun as the man stalked angrily by. The man shouted, "God, show me a miracle." And a precious baby was born, but the man didn't pay attention. So he said once again, "Let me know You are here, God . . . touch my arm." Just then, the man impatiently brushed away the beautiful butterfly that was sitting on his shoulder.

Don't miss out on the blessings all around you. Things are not always what they seem. God speaks to us through the tiniest ant, the soft voice of a true friend's sincere encouragement, and the cooing of a dove. He whispers in our heart, "Be at peace," and lets us know He is here. God is just an awareness away.

There are miracles happening every day; all we have to do is believe it. Clear out the channels of your mind and make way for them! You can look and see Him with eyes of faith. As a poet once said, "Blind unbelief is sure to err and scan his work in vain. God is His own interpreter and He will make it plain."

Keep your heart clear and bright. It is the window through which you see the world.

How could the great astronomers observe the workings of the heavens without the lenses of their mighty telescopes being cleansed continually? I recall the Bible saying, "Touch not the unclean thing and I will receive you and be a Father unto you."

Do you want to see God? Do you want an audience with the King of Kings? You cannot impatiently and angrily demand His presence. You are the one who must prepare a place for Him. Look around your dwelling place. Is there that which He would call unclean? Remember the condition of your reception by Him. He wants to be a Father to you, but first, you must throw out the trashy magazines and censor certain computer Web sites and television programs. You know which ones.

If there is something within you calling for God, it is only because He desires to talk to you, to love you, to give you peace. Prepare a place for Him as you would prepare your home to receive the greatest guest you can imagine.

So you must prepare your heart for Him, for He will not only walk into the living room, He will also sit down in the dining room and partake of your food and the music you listen to. He will be there when you sleep, and as you sleep He will begin to open the closets of your mind and observe how you have clothed yourself.

For His one and only purpose is to once again restore the lovely innocence and joy He put into you as a little child and restore you once and for all as His dear child—cared for, loved, and protected by angels and miracles.

Take notice . . . during raging, stormy nights the little birds huddle down in their nests. Safe and secure, the birds are protected when even mighty oaks fall. If God feeds and protects the tiniest sparrow, just think of how much more than that He cares for you. He will hold you in the shelter of His arms. All you have to do is make clear and clean the way He must enter your heart.

Don't Stop Believing in Miracles

As I concentrate on each word of this essay, seconds meld into hours as the future unfolds with every day passing. If yesterday is gone and tomorrow is not yet, then today is of the utmost importance. We must make a conscious decision to make our days glorious. The future only improves as we make the choice to make this day our absolute best.

A brighter tomorrow grows out of a sunnier and faith-filled today, so I make this choice: "This is the day that the Lord has made, I will [put all of my determination to] rejoice and be glad in it." —Psalm 118–24 and "I will hear what the Lord will speak for . . . The Lord shall give what is good . . . "—Psalm 85.

Our days are full of promise, stacked high with potential and over-flowing with joy. Moments are like scrolls; you can write on them what you want to be remembered.

Make the best out of your circumstances. Ask God early each morning to be the motivation behind every action, word, or thought. We are here on this good earth for a reason. God has predestined plans for our life. He created us to fulfill a purpose in His great design.

Each moment is a miracle. A miracle is any moment that is filled with the wonder of the revelation of God's intervention, an extraordinary event that can't be explained. Anticipate miracles and they will happen.

God certainly does answer prayer. He will take charge of one's life if invited in, and when that seed starts to grow in the heart, it flowers and blossoms and never stops growing.

I have a friend whose car was very old. She didn't have a husband to fix it or finances to repair it. Each day before she had to travel miles to work, she would get in the car and lay her hands on the dashboard and pray, "Thank You, Heavenly Father, for this car. You know I have a need of it to get me safely to work and back again. Please keep it running for me. In Jesus' name I ask it."

Each day, day after day, month after month, though it rattled and smoked, the car got her to work and back. One day she surprised herself by adding to her prayer, "And Lord, if it is Your will, I know You can give me a new car even though I have no money to buy one. Thank You so much."

Well, you know what happened. A few months later her son said, "Mom, I've got a part for your car that will make it run great." As he handed her a car-parts box, he said, "Look in it." She opened the box and there was a key. He took her outside and there was a new car. Her son and brother got together and bought her a car completely paid for. This was a miracle of answered prayer to my friend. Don't miss those miracles that are disguised in what may seem a logical outcome. They are still miracles.

I read in Proverbs 4:18, "The paths of right living people are as a shining light: that shines more and more until the perfect day." Choose to mold your life into God's plans. Reach new heights with trust and faith. Give all to Him.

Success comes, for me, in saying and believing the word "can." From now on, boost your confidence by saying, "I can win," "I can achieve," "I can do all things through Jesus Christ who strengthens me." "All things are possible if you believe." "Faith is the substance of things hoped for, the evidence (fact) of things unseen."

Remember, God promises to supply all of our needs, so believe in miracles. They happen all over the world . . . every day.

Achieve Destiny a Bit Higher Than Earth

E nglish novelist Edward Bulwer-Lytton wrote, "We are born for a higher destiny than that of earth. There is a realm where the rainbow never fades, where the stars will be spread out before us like islands that slumber on the ocean and where the beings that now pass before us, like shadows, will stay in our presence forever."

Achieve a higher destiny for yourself and your loved ones right here on this beautiful planet we call earth. Joy, success, contentment, and peace are all available to you now no matter what situation you may be in or where you are in life.

Did you ever go on a car trip and, after driving along for a while, realize you were lost? You stopped and asked for directions at a service station and found out that you were not too far off course after all and continued on to your destination. In your journey through life, though you may have gotten lost and wandered off the course a bit, it's not too late to begin anew and to take the right directions to get on the right path.

As we pass through this world together, let's do what we know deep in our hearts to be right. I often think of the quote, "I shall pass through this world only once. Any good therefore that I can do, or any kindness that I can show to any human being, let me do it now. Let me not defer or neglect it, for I shall not pass this way again." Let's follow the directions of the great Map Maker of life, who knows the simplest way to the eternal city, atop the mountain of God.

Have love in your heart. No matter what life has dealt you, "Love the Lord your God with all your heart, and with all your soul, and with all your strength, and with all your mind; and your neighbor as yourself." —Luke 10:27. Look on all things with love; be patient and kind. Know that hate only grows out of fear. So trust in God.

See the handiwork of God in the tiniest snowflake and the grandest sunset. Look to nature to express His beauty and majesty.

Do something nice for someone every day, as you would have them do for you. It could be a simple smile or a basket of goodies. Charity is love in action.

Speak kindly. We can do so much good through the words that we speak. Words of encouragement, faith, and understanding can help to transform a life. Do not waste your time or energy on menial, unimportant things. Negativity, hostility, jealousy, and strife can ruin everything about you. Guard your life. Your hours are too valuable to be wasted on worrying about what might happen, or someone's spiteful ways. Don't let anyone or anything rain on your parade.

Fulfill your own special dreams. Your potential is unlimited. Don't follow the herd or listen to the naysayers. You can have your heart's desire and live the life you've always imagined. Aim high, work hard, and master the art of patience, because anything of value takes time to complete.

Be thankful for the gift of today. Welcome each morning with a smile of appreciation for another chance at success. Let the wisdom of God's Word and prayer set the tone for the entire day. Yesterday has passed, and today's precious hours spent with loved ones are full of new opportunities and exciting possibilities. Remember: We are seated in Heavenly places, far above all principalities and powers. Be not conformed to the image of this world's media. Be conformed to the Master Map Maker and you will joyfully reach your destination.

The Emperor Penguin

Never underestimate the importance of a good father. After laying her single egg, the female emperor penguin leaves her nest to feed. It is then that the male emperor penguin incubates the egg by himself.

The male cradles the small egg between the top of his feet and his stomach for two long months. Papa penguin sits on the icy cold ground with temperatures as frigid as 40 degrees below zero, warming and protecting that precious egg.

During that entire time, the male emperor does not eat. By the time the egg hatches, the father has lost a third of his body weight. When the female returns to care for the baby, the male heads to the water for food and rest.

What an amazing example God has given us in nature of an unselfish and totally dedicated father.

So let us give tribute to loving, caring, and faithful fathers—men who say, as I read that Job said, "I have esteemed thy word greater than my necessary food."

A good dad is many things: a role model, an advisor, teacher, and godly example. Children are led best by positive example, not words. Many of us owe our confidence, courage, and faith to the encouragement of our dads.

A recent study by the Department of Education suggests that when dads play an active role in their children's education, grades go up. Researchers ranked dads' participation in school activities, going to class events, volunteering in the school, and attending parent-teacher conferences high on the list of making children real achievers in life. Further studies suggest that when a father attends these functions, his child is more likely to enjoy school, participate in extracurricular activities, and do well academically.

Research also states that when fathers demonstrate approval and warmth and give plenty of attention to their children, they produce self-reliant, mature girls and confident, skillful boys. Daughters, for example, did better at school when their fathers played sports with them and cheered on their earnest attempts. "If you can compete on the tennis court, then you probably can be a real competitor in the courtroom," one dad said.

Boys benefit from nurturing fathers, too, learning by example how to be a real man and a caring and compassionate husband someday. By taking a sincere interest in their friends, helping them with their home-work, and playing games with them, fathers can lead their children to a better understanding of what sterling character is. For recreation, some fathers and sons play chess together. Chess is a good game to instill in your child the need to think before you jump or make a move to do anything.

A good father can give the great gift of persistence to his children. He can dry their tears, comfort them, and help them to overcome and succeed by continually saying, "I know you can do it," and "Just try and try again."

I think that dads really need to read the Book of Proverbs in the Bible with their children. It is full of wisdom, and you will never be at a loss as to what to say to your child.

We all have the need for a loving and devoted father. For those of us who no longer have an earthly father, remember that you do have a won-derful Heavenly Father. It is God, and He loves and values you as His greatest treasure and precious child. He has written a whole book telling of His great love for you. Pick it up and read it, and be transformed into "A New You."

God Works in Mysterious Ways

I was sitting in my office last week, answering some of the wonderful and heartwarming letters from you, my dear readers.

As I opened a floral-printed card, there was a request and a self-addressed, stamped envelope: "Thank you for your article entitled, 'Give thanks before taking God's gifts.' Please send me another copy. I want to send this present one to my nephew in Virginia who graduates from college soon. It was just the article I needed in my life at the moment, and I am sure it will be appreciated by my nephew."

I thought to myself, "I wonder which column she is referring to?" Each newspaper tops each column with a different headline, so there was no way of knowing which one she meant.

I put her sweet card down on the desk. Something within me just knew that God would take care of it, so I just continued going through my stack of mail.

The very last letter I opened was from a lady who wished to express her appreciation for a certain column, and enclosed with her precious letter was a copy of the column titled, "Give thanks before taking God's gifts."

I had to laugh with delight in the Lord's wonderful ways! I took the column and immediately placed it in the self-addressed envelope and sent it off with love. How wonderfully God supplied that need, one for the other, unknown to each other. "The steps [actions, words, and deeds] of a good man are ordered by the Lord." —Psalm 37:23.

It seems like a paradox, impossible but true, but time and time again, God controls our lives. There are little miracles happening all around us, things that boggle the mind and delight the soul. Open your heart to them and know that He cares for you. The moment you put your life in God's hands, your transformation begins. Just wait and see what He gives.

Keep a booklet of your own life's little miracles. Record the small events and testimonies of God's intervention and provision. Bit by bit, as you read and reread the miraculous works God performs in your life, fear fades away, worry disappears, and you know that God has and will supply all of your needs. If God does so many small miracles, then the really big ones are just as easy for Him.

A miracle is defined as "an event that appears unexplainable by the laws of nature and so is held to be supernatural or an act of God." A reader wrote via e-mail, "I am in the navy right now in support of the 'Operation Allied Forces' here in the Adriatic Sea. Last night I was at the mess deck and I found your article. I have no idea how it got into the ship. The article title is 'Give thanks before receiving the gifts of God,' and I want to thank you for writing such an article. You have encouraged me to never lose my desire to triumph no matter what the situation is in the world. God always helps us."

When you have great faith, no matter how small the incident, you are rewarded. God answers that perfect faith. God can do exceedingly above and abundantly beyond all that we ask or think. But we must have faith and trust in Him.

There may be little things that we are momentarily inspired to do, but day by day we think we are doing just ordinary things. However, God is directing us. When our thoughts are to please others, doing kind deeds, God will not let our good actions go for naught.

I know there is a Scripture that says, "Cast your bread upon the water, it will return to you after many days." And I read another that says, "Be not weary in doing good for in due season we will reap if we faint not."

Look, dear readers, how you have blossomed. You have lifted yourself into the realm where all things are possible. Your letters tell me so.

Together we have learned to revere God's Word. We know how precious it is to Him that we are willing to live for Him by caring for others. There are no coincidences with God. There are just small miracles.

Angels Walk Among Us Each and Every Day

If our spiritual eyes could be opened, we would see that there are angels among us. They are about 7 feet tall—beautiful, strong angels—and they walk with us wherever we go, guarding us at home, at work, and at play.

They protect us, one on each side of our being, guarding us with their fiery swords drawn, just like the great warriors that they are. And as I read in the Bible, "We are surrounded by a great cloud of witnesses."

A reader wrote, "My husband and I were trying to clean our driveway of snow. Some big fellow in a red pickup truck with a snow blade started at the street where the snowplow had pushed about four feet of snow across our property and blocked our driveway. The stranger put his snow blade against that bank of snow and just kept on until he had our whole driveway cleared. That dear man just gave us a wave and left. We didn't get to thank him, but we prayed that God would bless him. I think he was an angel." I've heard that angels never wait around for thanks; they know all the glory goes to God.

Where love abounds, angels hover overhead. With or without being seen, they are present, directed by the Holy Spirit, a loving glow beside us, keeping us safe and warm.

Angels give us comfort, confidence, and guidance according to God's direction. "For He shall give His angels charge over thee to keep thee in all thy ways."—Psalm 91:11.

Angels are ministers of grace sent by the Father. Hear the rush of their wings as we praise Him. When we lift our voices in praises and song, the room gets so crowded. In the spiritual world, beams of God's light shine up into space, the angels see them, and they come swiftly, calling to each other to gather around and join in our praise.

I once read a story about a young man who, on a racing bike, started riding downward on a winding, steep mountain road. When he tried to apply his brakes, they failed. Faster and faster the man sped out of control. On one side of him was a steep drop; on the other side, solid rock. Frozen in fear, he prayed, "God, help me!" Suddenly he felt immediately calm. As he looked up, he saw and heard about twenty angels flying along with him, calmly talking and laughing with each other. The angels were just joyously doing their job. The next thing he knew was that he was safely stopped at the bottom of the hill. That young man's eyes were opened for a split second into the spiritual world.

There were many incidences of angels seen in the battle during World Wars I and II. We do not see angels all the time because our walk here on earth is to be a walk of faith. With that strong faith, we can conquer all obstacles and know we have angels to help us. "Faith is the substance of things hoped for the evidence of things not seen."—Hebrews 11:1.

In desperate times some people are allowed a glimpse of the angels. But day by day, we can know in our hearts what our eyes can't see. You can't see love, but you know when it's there; you can't see joy, but you feel it in your heart. Gravity has never been seen, but we live in the effect of it every day. It is the same thing with the presence of angels.

Music is said to be the speech of angels. And when I sing to my daughters about God's goodness, I can almost see the angels that gather around us and join in with us in singing His praises. In the softness of the evening, when I sing to them the lullabies of God's love, they fall asleep with a smile on their sweet faces and I think of the quote by Longfellow: "Silently one by one, in the infinite meadows of heaven / Blossomed the lovely stars, the forget-me-nots of angels."

Pain and Hardship Serve Purposes in Our Lives

Have you ever walked in the midst of a beautiful, lush forest . . . and suddenly come upon a stark rock quarry? Here the lovely earth has been scarred, where great machines broke away the big chunks of rocks and left the forest to heal itself.

Let us ponder the similar circumstances in our lives. Perhaps pain and hardship serve the same purpose in human beings. Maybe the trials that have scarred our lives have really helped us develop a sense of direction so that we may ultimately reach the destination intended for us.

When an artist gets a block of marble delivered, it is just a large, rough chunk of rock. The artist sits and broods over it until within it he sees something, a revelation in his heart and mind, and he knows he can bring forth beauty out of that hard, cold stone. As he diligently works, with strikes of chisel and hammer, great chunks drop to the floor in broken pieces. But after weeks, months, and even years, the stone takes shape and form and becomes a masterpiece of beauty.

Out of difficulties come the opportunities for tremendous growth, wisdom, and patience. Tough times can turn into strength of character, healing, and deepening love. Learn from the pains of yesterday and forget the failures. No matter what mistakes you have made, God forgives and forgets. A new life can begin for you today. The storms we experience certainly will not cease, but by the grace of God you can choose to rise above them.

If you had a child to raise into mature adulthood, with fine character and full of wisdom, would you let the child have its way all the time? Would you let that child eat candy for every meal because it tastes good? Would you let that child play all the time because it's fun? Of course, if you really loved that child, the answer must be "no."

Remember, God is a Father and He allows hard times to come into our lives for the same reason we make our children eat vegetables, clean their rooms, and do their chores. Character is not a gift; it is a victory. He has a purpose in allowing these things. We can't run away if something happens that throws us. Take a deep breath and try to understand the reason God allowed it.

Things are going to happen to us in our lives all along the way. We must not act rashly. If we pause and think, perhaps we can see the good that can come out of the situation. Sometimes things seem so dark, and we don't see what God is doing. No matter the circumstance, let the Word of God work in you.

You have seen with your eyes the works of the greatest Artist, painted over the sky at sunset. Respect Him as He allows the chisel and hammer to deliver its blows upon your life. Don't hang your head down, staring at the broken pieces. Lift up your eyes to Him. Thank God at every opportunity, for when you put your faith completely in Him, He will take care of your needs more wonderfully than you could ever ask.

Trust in God's goodness and follow where He leads. For if you wait in love and patience and let Him shape you, one day you will know that you yourself have become His masterpiece . . . an object of grace, beauty, and love . . . a reflection of the Master Himself.

Thank Heavens for People Like Denise

It was about three o'clock in the afternoon of September 11, 2001, when the doorbell rang.

I looked outside and saw a young lady standing at my front step. As I opened the door, she said, smiling, "Hi, I'm Denise." Then, holding out her hand, she gave me something and said, "This is yours."

I looked down in question and saw that she was holding my wallet. She explained, "I found this wallet in a cart outside the grocery store this afternoon and wanted to return it to you."

Surprised, I recalled that earlier that day, I did go to the grocery store to pick up diapers for the children. "I can't believe it," I said in shock. "I never even realized the wallet was lost because of the day's tragic happenings. Thank you so much." She even refused the reward I offered! How beautiful is an honest heart; what a decent, good, and kind deed. When I think that someone could have found the wallet and not returned it, I thank God for people like her.

It's wonderful that there are people who believe in honesty. They just do what's right naturally, and I'm inclined to think that these are the majority. I believe in the saying, "What goes around, comes around." What you are comes back to you.

It is important to observe and consider before you react. It's amazing how fast our minds work and why we come to the conclusions that we do. In a fraction of a second we choose right over wrong, or vice versa.

Our reaction to an action reveals the truth. How do we react in a split second? What has control over our life? Out of the motivations of the heart come the determination to think and do right. What's in the core of your heart? Therein lies what gives us peace or restlessness.

If you ever decide to give God more time in your life, you had better be prepared for battle. In fact, it's a real eye opener to the fact of God's existence. The proof is in the opposing forces in this battle. It seems as though everything will come against you to keep you from prayer or reading the Word. But believe me, it is worth it. Time is never lost that is spent with God.

I find that the Word of God is my peace and my guide. I can turn to it and find the right solution to every problem. If I give the situation to God in prayer, He can put the right thoughts in my mind. I know if I look to Him before I react to anything, God can guide me. In a split second, my subconscious mind calls on Him. I can hear Him say, "Don't worry, my child, I will be faithful in my promises to guide you." Then I can cast all my fears and worries on Him. We can travel on this road of life without fear.

A dear friend of mine told me of a dream she had years ago. She dreamed that she was a child, walking through a field with God holding her hand. This was a state of ideal perfection. Then He stopped and looked at her and said, "My time is not your time. If you ever need me, call my name, and I will take you out of your time and into my time." All this would happen in a split second. And in a split second, it would remove fear or doubt. The answers to her questions would come clearly into focus.

The enemy trembles when a child of God gets down on their knees. Prayer can change things. We don't pray to change the mind of God; we pray so that He may change us. How sweet it is at the end of the day to look to God, to thank Him for loving us, guiding us, and for the bleach of His blood that washes away the stain of sin, and the power of His Word that overcomes all obstacles.

And He gives us the peace to lay our head on our pillows and sleep a deep restoring sleep . . . of faith.

Cherish These Moments and Give Thanks

Branches of giant oak trees seem to reach up to a universe full of possibilities as your arms reach out to me, dear child. I pick you up and embrace all the possibilities within you.

A mother eagle waits for her baby eagle to grow into its courage and live its dreams. With more faith than experience, the small eagle soars into the heavens. You, my little one, will fly to your dreams one day, and I will urge you onward toward your path.

But like the quiet inlets and coves up and down the rugged coast where seabirds come to rest when they tire, my heart will always be a shelter for you, my child, when you long to come home.

The large gulf of the river is wide and powerful, yet it began as a tiny, rushing stream. Like the bubbling brook, you are young and headed for a great God-inspired destiny that is all your own. What that destiny is I do not know, but if you should ever need me, in a heartbeat, always know that I will be there for you.

Whatever life brings, wherever you journey or call home, one thing will always be true: that you are a part of me and I, my dear daughters, am a part of you.

I think that at times, we are so busy with our daily chores, hectic schedules, and busyness that we forget what great gifts children really are.

"Rings and jewels are not gifts, but apologies for gifts. The only true gift is a portion of thyself."—Ralph Waldo Emerson.

Our time will always be short and our attention will always be distracted. So we must choose deliberately to make the time to give children the memories of our love. Giving children your undivided attention means love to them. Teach them to talk to God and to love Him with all their heart. And as your child sees your love, your tender care, so he or she will view God's love.

I know of a grandmother who made her first acquaintance of her grandson when he was five years old. The other set of grandparents had lots of money to buy the boy many gifts, but this grandmother did not. She prayed and asked God to let her show her grandson how much she loved him. Every time he came over, she would sit on the floor and play a game with him, or they would read a book together.

One day the little fellow looked up at her and said, "Grammy, you love me more than my other grandma." Quickly she stated, "Oh, I'm sure that's not true. I know they love you just as much as I."

But the boy shook his head.

The grandmother asked, "Why do you think this way?" The boy replied, "Because you always sit down and play with me."

Grammy said, "Your other grandmother is busy cleaning her house, and her home is cleaner than mine."

The little fellow shook his head again. "I don't care about that. You care about me."

Though a clean house is so important, undivided attention builds memories of love. So I make sure we make the time to take visits to the library and walks to the park. I listen to them giggle like the bubbling brook, read books to them before bedtime, and we say prayers together.

As I watch my two daughters sleeping, I smile at the precious gifts God has given us charge over. I don't want to let a minute go by without expressing my love to them. That is why I must now embrace the price-less time we have. And when we say our prayers at night, I say an extra one, too. I thank God for giving me these precious girls . . . and I rejoice to know they are gifts from Him.

Afterword

"Two roads diverged in a wood, and I—I took the one less traveled by, and that has made all the difference."—Robert Frost

About the Author

CATHERINE GALASSO-VIGORITO is the author of the syndicated weekly column, "A New You," which is hosted by *The New Haven Register* and appears in newspapers nationwide. She is a widely acclaimed writer who is renowned for her ability to uplift, encourage, and comfort her readers.

Catherine's other print accomplishments include contributions to *All About the Baby Magazine*, *The Connecticut Post Newspaper*, and *The Woodbridge Bulletin*, among others. She is also the author of the very successful, self-published: *The Treasure of a New You* (1998).

In addition, Catherine has garnered admiration for her work in television and radio. While representing Connecticut in the Miss USA pageant (1988) Catherine was also busy appearing in the daytime television shows *Loving* and *Another World*. Catherine fine-tuned her inspirational "new you" ideas in her live television segment of the same title which aired for a year on WTNH-News Channel 8 in Connecticut.

Currently Catherine works as an account executive for Clear Channel Radio. She lives in Branford, Connecticut, with her husband, Todd, and their two daughters, Lauren Grace and Gabriella Elise.